A Life Undone

A Father's Journey through Loss

Barry Kluger

iUniverse, Inc.
New York   Bloomington

A Life Undone
A Father's Journey through Loss

Copyright © 2010 Barry Kluger

All rights reserved. No part of this book may be used or reproduced by any means, graphic, electronic, or mechanical, including photocopying, recording, taping or by any information storage retrieval system without the written permission of the publisher except in the case of brief quotations embodied in critical articles and reviews.

iUniverse books may be ordered through booksellers or by contacting:

iUniverse
1663 Liberty Drive
Bloomington, IN 47403
www.iuniverse.com
1-800-Authors (1-800-288-4677)

Because of the dynamic nature of the Internet, any Web addresses or links contained in this book may have changed since publication and may no longer be valid. The views expressed in this work are solely those of the author and do not necessarily reflect the views of the publisher, and the publisher hereby disclaims any responsibility for them.

ISBN: 978-1-4502-0846-8 (pbk)
ISBN: 978-1-4502-0848-2 (cloth)
ISBN: 978-1-4502-0849-9 (ebook)

Library of Congress Control Number: 2010901522

Printed in the United States of America

iUniverse rev. date: 3/10/10

Erica Alexis Kluger
November 27, 1982-April 6, 2001
"You will dance in our hearts forever"
(headstone inscription)

Contents

Foreword ix
Acknowledgments xiii
"The Artist's Task" by Jack Riemer xvii
Introduction xxi

PART 1: A LIFE

Chapter 1:   Graveside: The Eulogy 3
Chapter 2:   Roots 6
Chapter 3:   In the Beginning, God Created Erica 8
Chapter 4:   Single Dad 12
Chapter 5:   Alone Together 16
Chapter 6:   The Paradigm Shift: A New Start 20
Chapter 7:   "You from Joisey? I'm from Joisey!" 23
Chapter 8:   Camp Danbee, 1994 29
Chapter 9:   Arizona and This Thing Called the Internet 32
Chapter 10: It-ly, Not Italy 34
Chapter 11: Hi Ho, Hi Ho 37
Chapter 12: Howdy, Pardner 40
Chapter 13: The Long, Hot Summer 44
Chapter 14: Prelude to a Loss 51

PART 2: UNDONE

Chapter 15: A Day Unlike Any Other 75
Chapter 16: The Morning After 81
Chapter 17: Passover and Palm Sunday: Faiths Converge ... 84
Chapter 18: A New Week 90

Chapter 19:	The Show	93
Chapter 20:	Shiva	97
Chapter 21:	Shiva Part Deux: Five Days without Erica	100
Chapter 22:	Florida Calls	104
Chapter 23:	The S—List	109
Chapter 24:	The Endless Summer	112
Chapter 25:	The Veil behind the Unveiling	117
Chapter 26:	The Dog Days of Summer	121
Chapter 27:	Up, Up and Away and a New Year Dawns	123
Chapter 28:	In Like a Lion	126
Chapter 29:	Summertime Blues 2002	133
Chapter 30:	Dimming of the Light	137
Chapter 31:	Halfway to Being an Orphan	140
Chapter 32:	A Pack of Marlboros and an Outstretched Hand	144
Chapter 33:	Death Touches a Friend	150
Chapter 34:	Closure? Perhaps	153
Chapter 35:	Erica Turns Twenty-seven: The Words of Others	159
Chapter 36:	2010: Looking Back	172

Foreword

Towards the end of February, I was connected to Barry through a mutual link of former teachers and students from Plainview, New York. When I researched further, I came to realize, we both shared the loss of a child, and both tragically in the beginning of what would have been wonderful lives.

40 years ago, on May 4, 1970, I lost my son, Jeffrey, who, along with three of his fellow classmates was shot to death by the Ohio National Guard in what has become one of the darkest episodes in our short history. In that thirteen-second burst of gunfire, nine other students were also wounded. They were protesting the Vietnam War and had been brought up to believe that they were guaranteed the right of free speech and could safely voice their objections to a war that they felt deeply was wrong. No one thought that those freedoms which made our country "special" could be taken away so abruptly.

Barry sent me a final draft of his book and as I read it, I came to understand that while loss affects us in so many different ways, there is indeed no "garden variety of death." I "spent the weekend" with

Barry Kluger

Barry, Erica and their many friends and family members and I felt I came to know them all so well.

Certain things stood out--saying that he had no one to be angry at - it was a car accident - nobody to blame. I'm not sure whether I was torn apart or somehow sustained by my fury - I had so many people to blame. I focused on Richard Nixon as the main culprit for his creating an atmosphere that permitted a branch of our government to shoot at unarmed students.

From the opening anecdote about Itzhak Perlman, all the way to this past December, his openness and honesty let me in - into his mind and heart and emotions - and, inevitably made me play back my own similar but different story. I was forever moved. I wasn't sure if I was mourning for Erica (or Jeff) or for him (or me).

A Life Undone exposed the commonalities and the differences we share. I'm grateful to Barry for pulling no punches since I, too, went through some of those worrisome teenage times.

His awareness that people were pointing him out as "the guy, whose daughter was killed," Oh yes, I remember that very well. And I shared the resentment toward the people who weren't there for us, who either avoided me or said some of those insensitive things he mentions. We both 'mourned' over those close to us who just didn't know how to find the words we needed them to say. I suspect we are both not quite over that yet.

A Life Undone is truly a celebration of sorts. It has helped me recognize the moments of joy in Jeffrey's short life and Erica's as well and I know this will be an inspiration to others. There are the moments of clarity, acceptance, resignation, anger and loss we all share and if it's possible to take this story and make our own time on earth that much more valuable and one to be cherished, then our children will not have died in vain.

-Elaine Miller Holstein, March 1, 2010

Acknowledgments

Writing this book was more of a celebration than a catharsis, because every word I wrote was an opportunity to think about Erica.

I'd like to thank the following friends and families who have been there through e-mails and phone calls and have offered many other signs of support starting from the day Erica was born until the day she died and then some.

Deborah Susser, my editor at the *Jewish News,* who took me to lunch in June 2009 and got me to finally sit down and write this book, going from eight thousand words to almost forty thousand in a matter of weeks.

The strangers who wrote me saying they read of my loss and just wanted to send some solace my way.

My editors at Gannett's *Arizona Republic,* who besides printing my usual rants and raves, gave me the opportunity to keep Erica alive through my columns.

Barry Kluger

Shannon, Erica's best friend, who was with her as a young girl and in her last few days here in Arizona; she has kept a light burning for Erica and carries the torch of her goodness every day.

Dr. Jeff McWhirter of Arizona State University, who counseled me on grief less than twenty-four hours after Erica died and guided me through the next few years.

Rabbi Ken Segel, who extended his hand and his healing in helping me make sense of something that made no sense at all.

Wall Street Journal columnist and author Jeffrey Zaslow, who allowed me to be part of a very important column on loss and for continuing to write stories of inspiration.

My friend Glenn, who bothered me every day to draw me out in the early days.

Mike from Laramie, Wyoming, and Eric from California, who found me on the Internet after their own losses and shared tears and laughs about children lost.

The people at Alive Alone, an organization that helps parents through the loss and keeps them alive in monthly newsletters.

Steven and Dana for being the best new friends in our new adopted home of Arizona and for not leaving us alone in the fell clutch of circumstance.

Meryl, who, while she hates to get on airplanes, was there every day for years to check in on me, and it was as if she was right by my side.

All my MTV friends and Erica's 'aunts,' Carole, Brett, Jodi, Linda, Renee, Judy, and especially my friend, Julie, who responded to my loss with love and kind words.

Steve Cohen, who got on a plane within hours of hearing of Erica's death and spent the next few weeks, months, and years being a true friend.

All my Plainview friends who came along through the process, especially at the time of Erica's death: Jill, Robin, Mindy, Marcie.

My dear friend, Mindy Cassel, who created the Children's Bereavement Center in Florida and mixed a healthy dose of professional expertise with forty years of friendship and love.

Gar (Gary) Mansfield, who was there like a brother, always calling and still calling as of this writing, to check on me.

Ira Steinberg for being on the first plane out after hearing of the tragedy.

Devon, Jenna, Holly, Katie, and all the others who contacted me in November to talk about Erica and share photos.

Lorraine who, with me, tried to make sense of something that has no logic and was honest in discussing with me the hurricane known as Erica.

Matthew, Zack, and Alley; may the memories not dim and may the pain turn into strength and resolve.

Alan, Amy, Jesse, Lisa, and Esther for seeing the good in Erica and reminding me of her light.

Lori, Jeff, Cutler, Aidan, and Joan for living through the tragedy and helping me come out on the other side.

Barry Kluger

My late parents, Lee and Len, especially Mom, for being so strong at a time I needed a shoulder. Their love of life was passed on to me, and I, in turn, passed that on to Erica.

My friend of more than fifty-three years, Walter, who was with me when Erica died and was a rock at a time I was jelly.

Carol: through our love, we created someone wonderful. And for that, I thank you.

Hope, who gave me a second chance at happiness. I will never be able to adequately express how much your words of gratitude and love got me through the darkest period anyone can ever face. The scratching of the back, the rustling of my hair, the knowing nod at the times when I would just sigh—your strength pulled me through it, and for that, I will be eternally grateful. You demonstrated that love conquers all.

And finally, you, Erica, for having graced my life. I am a better person for having had you in it. You taught me that through your love. The Tin Man said it best: "A heart is not measured by how much *you* love but by how much you are loved by others." My God, how you were loved.

"The Artist's Task"
by Jack Riemer

Published in *The Houston Chronicle (1995)*

Itzhak Perlman, the violinist, came on stage to give a concert at Avery Fisher Hall at Lincoln Center in New York City. If you have ever been to a Perlman concert, you know that getting on stage is no small achievement for him. He was stricken with polio as a child, and so he has braces on both legs and walks with the aid of two crutches. To see him walk across the stage one step at a time, painfully and slowly, is a sight. He walks painfully, yet majestically, until he reaches his chair.

Then he sits down, slowly, puts his crutches on the floor, undoes the clasps on his legs, tucks one foot back and extends the other foot forward. Then he bends down and picks up the violin, puts it under his chin, nods to the conductor, and proceeds to play.

The orchestra waits quietly while he makes his way across the stage to his chair. They remain reverently silent while he undoes the clasps on his legs. They wait until he is ready to play. But this time, something went wrong. Just as he finished the first few bars, one of the strings on his violin broke. You could hear it snap—it went off like gunfire across the room. There was no mistaking what that sound meant. There was no mistaking what he had to do.

People who were there that night thought to themselves: "We figured that he would have to get up, put on the clasps again, pick up the crutches and limp his way off stage—to either find another violin or else find another string for this one." But he didn't. Instead, he waited a moment, closed his eyes and then signaled the conductor to begin again.

The orchestra began, and he played from where he had left off. And he played with such passion and such power and such purity as they had never heard before. Of course, anyone knows that it is impossible to play a symphonic work with just three strings. I know that, and you know that, but that night Itzhak Perlman refused to know that.

You could see him modulating, changing, and recomposing the piece in his head. At one point, it sounded like he was detuning the strings to get new sounds from them that they had never made before. When he finished, there was an awesome silence in the room.

And then people rose and cheered. There was an extraordinary outburst of applause from every corner of the auditorium. We were all on our feet, screaming and cheering; doing everything we could to show how much we appreciated what he had done. He smiled, wiped the sweat from this brow, raised his bow to quiet us, and then he said, not boastfully, but in a quiet, pensive, reverent tone,

"You know, sometimes it is the artist's task to find out how much music you can still make with what you have left."

What a powerful line that is. It has stayed in my mind ever since I heard it. And who knows? Perhaps that is the way of life—not just for artists but for all of us. Here is a man who has prepared all his life to make music on a violin of four strings, who, all of a sudden, in the middle of a concert, finds himself with only three strings. So he makes music with three strings, and the music he made that night with just three strings was more beautiful, more sacred, more memorable, than any that he had ever made before, when he had four strings.

So, perhaps our task in this shaky, fast-changing, bewildering world in which we live is to make music, at first with all that we have, and then, when that is no longer possible, to make music with what we have left.

(Reprinted with permission, 2010)

Introduction

Grief is a team sport. It takes many players to reach a common goal, and along the way there are botched plays, missed opportunities, and near wins.

Men grieve differently than women. The loss of a child is so outside the accepted lifecycle, and too often societal pressures and expectations muddy the waters.

My daughter, Erica, died on April 6, 2001, a year that carries a different distinction for me than for most Americans.

It took me almost nine years to write this book. In writing it, I had a wealth of material to draw from, not only my recollections of the experiences and my journals since 1974, but the e-mails following Erica's death. As a journalist for the *Arizona Republic,* I wrote columns about my loss, and those columns connected me to a network of other fathers across the country: to name two, Mike from Laramie and Eric from Boise each found some kind of solace in my writings. This opened up my eyes to how each loss is different and how certain circumstances help us heal.

Barry Kluger

Erica was in a car accident. She didn't commit suicide; she wasn't hit by a drunk driver; she didn't suffer a fatal overdose; and she wasn't the victim of a violent crime. She simply got into a crash. Maybe that loss was better than most since I had no one to be angry at—a DUI cruiser or someone who'd had his license revoked—and I had to deal with an all-too-common garden-variety death. Maybe the "simplicity" of the way it happened helped me focus on life without Erica. Maybe. Some of the others I've spoken with weren't so lucky.

May others learn from me, feel something from me, and cherish what we have, and pray to God every day. If one person's life is eased by reading my story, then I have accomplished something wonderful.

The Talmud says, "Whoever saves a life, it is considered as if he saved an entire world."

PART 1: A LIFE

Chapter 1

Graveside: The Eulogy

We know what to do when we lose a job. We know what to do when we have a flat tire. We know what to do when we see someone in trouble. We don't know what to do when we lose a child. No one, nothing, not even our faith prepares us for what we have to do, or feel. Sometimes, we don't feel at all, and we feel bad when we don't cry. And when we do cry, we feel it's not enough.

The Hebrew word *beshert* means, loosely translated, fate or "meant to be." We use the word when we meet someone and think we were destined to be together. But I don't understand it when a child dies and we are supposed to say it was fate, part of a grand plan, or that there is a "reason."

There are a lot of things I don't understand right now. I don't understand a lot of the things I am feeling, or not feeling. But I do know I miss Erica.

Saturday, I went to a meeting to tell the people there that Erica had died the day before. I said, "I know in this group there is anonymity and we use first names only, but my daughter's name was Erica Kluger." Remember that name.

We all know how much she was loved. I loved her more than I can ever say. They say a father's love for his daughter cannot be described in words ... I cannot find the words. The love is in my smile when I think of her, in my tears when I think of her, in my laugh when I think of her. I will forget when the dishwasher is not emptied and wonder why Erica forgot to do it, and then I will stop and remember why. And give anything to have her back.

She was the real product of two people, Carol and me. And the amalgam of all of you here today, friends and family alike.

Let me tell you about her. She would walk into a room and light it up. She used all of the bad jokes I had used that had been passed down from my father. Erica would get on the phone with my folks, and when my dad asked if she took a shower, she'd answer, "Why, is there one missing?" She talked about oodles and oodles of Chinese noodles with my mom, and she and my wife, Hope, loved to have Indepth discussions as to who was better, Kate Spade or Tommy Hilfiger, but she loved the time she had with Hope—the palling around, the talks, and the lectures—all of which helped build her character. She would talk about her brother, Zach, the poet; her sister, Alley, the dancer; her stepdad, Matt, the guy who played Beatles songs; and her mom, Carol ... well ... that was a love that was as deep as any I have seen.

We had the best month we could have hoped for. Her friend, Shannon, saved her life and gave her back to us for a brief period, to start to become the kind of person she wanted to be, could be, and was well on her way to being. I can't begin to thank you, Shannon.

She was a child who was immensely loved by what today we call *blended* families, with loads of extended relatives who came to know her and love her, and she knew that. In the past month, her life was finally coming together. She was making it and then … fate stepped in.

I said earlier I didn't know what I was feeling. Intellectually, I know. Hurt, sadness, anger and, in the next few days, months, and for the rest of my life, I will have to make sense of this jumble of emotions.

Someone said, as we get older, we start to know all the questions; we just don't have all the answers. I wish I knew the answer to Why?

I will remember Erica forever, and I ask that you do the same. A friend of mine said, "Don't let people tell you it will take time." We should not let time heal all wounds. We have all been wounded, hurt, and saddened, and if we let time heal, we will forget Erica, and that is something we must never do.

I ask of all of you here today to do Erica a favor. Tonight, walk down the halls and hug your kids goodnight, or if they are away at school or living on their own, pick up the phone and tell them you love them. Tell them about a little girl named Erica who wanted to grow up to be a dancer. And may she inspire them to be whatever they want to be.

She inspired me to be a better father, husband, son, and friend.

Erica, thank you for gracing my life.

—Eulogy for Erica Alexis Kluger by her father,
Barry Kluger,
April 10, 2001

Chapter 2

Roots

I grew up in Plainview, Long Island, one of those New York towns that sprang up in the early fifties, a mecca for on-the-rise families from Queens and beyond, who had either outgrown their two-bedroom apartments in Glen Oaks or traveled east for the promises of a plot of land stretching from Bethpage to Levittown.

I was barely two when I arrived, with a street, a neighborhood, a backyard, a dog, and a brother, not listed in an order reflecting my fondness for these things. Plainview was still farmland, and from the backyards one could see to the Miller place where Mid-Island Plaza would rise some eight years later. The population came from a mix of different cultures. Most were hardworking folks who were employed at the local Grumman Aircraft plant or were carving out careers at Central General Hospital—at a time when saving lives took precedence over saving for a late-model Benz or a home south of the highway—or labored in the garment center or at other occupations in Manhattan, some thirty-five minutes away.

We were a typical middle-class Jewish family, my dad having grown up in the rough East New York neighborhood of Brooklyn, my mom, the only child of comfortable parents who owned a couple of service stations. My dad, having lost his father at an early age, lived with a younger brother and older half-brother. We never did find out the sordid secrets of Grandmother Nettie's past. Nettie had been one tough broad, who scared the crap out of me because she rarely smiled. Clearly, her life had not been easy.

We were never close with my father's family, though my older cousins, Ronnie and Carol, had followed us with their folks to Plainview, just around the corner. My father and my Uncle Sid were in business together, running a philately company in New York for clientele that included Officer Joe Bolton, host of the *Three Stooges* show on Channel 11. My other uncle, Harold, had stayed in Brooklyn with his wife, Shirley, and their two sons, Ira and Michael, who could recite the Hebrew alphabet backwards and forwards. I was not planning to be a rabbi.

My mother's side was the exciting half of the equation, with a very large extended family, some of whom had perished in the Holocaust. Most of the ones who had survived were certifiably wacky. There was never a dull moment. One time, my cousin David showed up for Passover in a priest's collar, announcing, with an odd look in his eye, that he had joined a new religious order. After a Barucha and genuflection, dinner was served. But they were, after all, family.

I have cousins I saw only on holidays, and over the years, none of us did much to keep the family together. We learned over time that friends become like family, and such relationships have endured.

Chapter 3

In the Beginning, God Created Erica

Erica was born on November 27, 1982, at New York Hospital in Manhattan. Carol and I had been married for a little more than four years and were living in a luxury apartment building that had once been a single-room occupancy welfare hotel. Our Upper West Side one-bedroom was rather spacious by New York standards, with a full kitchen, walk-in closet, and a dining area that made a great alcove for a crib and Marimekko wallpaper trim with matching bedspreads. Erica's crib was the one Carol had slept in as an infant, and though I'm sure it would not have passed 1982 safety regulations, my father-in-law, Marvin, kept everything in the house in working and safe condition.

I hesitated to write about Erica's life before my divorce in 1987, but so much of the good she had in her was the result of having had two parents, each with unique qualities and gifts, not to mention an extended family that influenced her later on. As time went on, the trials and tribulations of that time faded from memory, and it would serve no purpose to try to make heroes and villains out of the people in Erica's life. Though her life was torn apart by our divorce, she was fortunate to live within two families who wanted only the best for her.

Carol was working as a textile designer in 1982, and I was heading up public relations at USA Networks, a twenty-four-hour sports and entertainment cable channel. I was on a career track in the media industry, and we were living a nice life in Manhattan, commuting to Glen Rock, New Jersey, each day. We both had families that were strong influences in Erica's life. Carol visited her dad and younger sisters, Andra and Debbie, across the river, first in Clifton and then North Brunswick. Over the years, we took trips to Florida, to visit my folks and to go to Disney World, which I suspect was even more fun for me than it was for Erica. (I love that place to this day! In fact, I wanted to spend my honeymoon with my second wife, Hope, at Epcot Center, but Hope had different ideas.)

When Erica was an infant, Carol and I took her wherever we went, to see friends and to eat at fine restaurants, getting a kick out of how Carol dressed her up. Carol surmised, correctly, that if Erica learned to be around grown-ups at an early age, she would relate more easily to adults later on.

In July of 1983, we bought our first house—in Tenafly, New Jersey, a well-to-do suburb. We followed the standard advice that says buy the worst home in the best location: we found an inexpensive home in one of the best towns on the Hudson. It was a small Dutch Colonial on a quiet street, the perfect place for Erica to grow up. We didn't have much money, but Carol made it a home, and Erica had her own room with a view to the street. We made friends in Tenafly, thanks to Carol's getting involved in the community through the JCC, where Erica went to preschool. Our life was different from that of many others in our town. I remember a class at the JCC that was called How to Handle Your Live-in Help. In our case, *we* were the live-in help.

We both worked. Carol was freelancing as a designer, working from home, and I commuted to my job at USA Network in Manhattan by bus every day. In the evening, I would call Carol and tell her what bus I was taking and when I would be getting off. When the bus pulled away, she and Erica would be standing on the corner, waiting for me to cross the street. This was America as I had imagined it.

We took advantage of everything the area had to offer, from the Tenafly Duck Pond (where two cooks were arrested one day, hunting for ducks for the local Chinese restaurant) to the Bronx Zoo. It was a perfect childhood.

One night, we heard Erica crying and went into her room to see what the matter was. We *heard* her but could not *see* her. It reminded me of a *Twilight Zone* episode in which a young girl fell behind a wall into a parallel universe. We finally found her wedged between the bed and the wall. That would be one of the many adventures we all would have.

There was also the night she was crying and we went into her room without turning on the light. We felt that the bed was wet and assumed that she had had an accident. But when we finally did turn on the light, we saw the bed was covered with blood. We rushed her to Englewood Hospital less than a mile away and found out that during the night, she had stuck her finger into her nose, breaking a blood vessel.

I'll never forget the day Erica was running down Oak Street with a tree branch in her hand, only to fall onto a twig. We took a flashlight, tilted her head back, and noticed a hole in the top palate of her mouth. We took her to the hospital yet again, and after being told this would heal over, we went home to continue our life with a mischievous four-year-old.

Over the next four years, Carol and I would start to have problems in our marriage—partly due to money but mostly due to my immaturity. I had gotten married at an early age, and while Carol clearly knew what she wanted—a nice suburban life, a family, a home—I didn't have as clear a picture of my needs and wants. It was this lack of commitment on my part that led to the breakup, and I became a person I was not very proud of.

Chapter 4

Single Dad

Carol and I split up the spring of 1987. The day I left, Carol drove me to the Teaneck Loew's Glenpointe Hotel, where I picked up a rental car to drive into the city. Erica sat in the back seat and cried, "Don't go!"

To say it was tough on Erica was an understatement. She now had to alternate her weekends, spending every other one with her mom and her mom's soon-to-be husband, Matt, and the alternate weekends with me in Manhattan. I began dating but chose not to introduce any of the women I socialized with to Erica, lest she get attached. I was not ready for a commitment but was open to it should it come along.

I was now a vice president at Viacom's MTV Networks and had a hectic travel schedule. Along with the position came free and easy VIP access to movies, concerts, and the like, giving Erica an entrée into an exciting world of culture that few kids even knew existed. I got to be, as her stepdad put it, the "fun dad," whereas he and Carol had to deal with the day-to-day issues, discipline, and, eventually, her rebellion.

Such was the life that became my routine. And Erica adapted to it reluctantly. I would make all my social arrangements for the weekends on which I didn't have her. On the weekends I did have her, I devoted all my time to her, taking her out to enjoy the bustling nightlife of New York, bringing her to places where couples sat drinking wine while Erica and I played.

In the summer of 1987, I lived in my friend Curt's condo, which was in an old church on West 11th Street that had been converted into a loft-like haven. Having Erica in the Village was as fun as could be. There were street fairs, festivals, parks, and tons of great restaurants. I planned things to do for every weekend, and we would spend the Friday nights watching TV, playing games, and settling in at about 11:00 PM

My work required me to spend a lot of time on the road, primarily in Los Angeles, and I would work those trips around Erica the best I could, keeping continuity in her life. I made sure I spoke to her every night. But sometimes I would get caught up in my busy schedule and would call the East Coast only to find out she was already in bed and I had to wait till the next day to hear her voice. It killed me not to talk to her.

Early in 1988, I moved from Curt's place to an apartment on East 35th Street between Park and Lexington avenues—a large one bedroom with a dining room, kitchen alcove, and a pull-out couch for Erica. It was a great neighborhood, a few blocks west of the East River. It was close to a skating rink that we enjoyed on Saturdays. There was also a temple across the street, which, from time to time, Erica and I would attend, to give her a little faith, or more important, cultural identity.

One of the things Erica liked to do was play talk show host. She would take a tape recorder and interview me for *The Erica Kluger Show*, as

I recreated the cartoon voices of characters I had loved as a child: Snagglepuss, Quick Draw McGraw, Yogi Bear, BooBoo and, of course, Babalooey.

Carol and I were divorced in February of 1988. She and Matt moved from Tenafly to Port Jefferson, on Long Island, which meant I was no longer thirty-five minutes away by bus. It was now a matter of two hours, at best, by car on the Long Island Expressway (LIE), which meant I needed to have a car in the city. I worked it out that I would leave work on "Erica weekends" at 3:00 PM, get out to her at about 5:00, and get back into the city by about 7:00, meaning she would often sleep in the car and then I'd wake her up so that she would begin her evening when most five-year-olds were getting ready for bed.

On 32nd Street, there was a small Greek diner (all the best ones in New York are Greek) where they loved seeing Erica on weekends. They used to let her talk into the microphone to call in orders to the kitchen. Imagine a six-year-old shouting, "Adam and Eve on a raft and wreck 'em" (scrambled eggs on toast) or "Walk a cow past the stove and cry on it" (hamburger rare with onions). That was always one of the highlights for her. Luckily for us, we were two blocks from the Empire State Building, which became a regular haunt: we'd marvel at the etchings of the Seven Wonders of the World in the lobby.

Erica became a regular at MTV, running into the offices of her "uncles," Dwight, Tom, and Marshall, whether or not they were in meetings. They would stop what they were doing, put a phone call on hold, and hang out. She had that effect on people. A CEO to her was a guy to draw pictures with. My department would get excited when she came to work. They always knew when it was her birthday. One year, she was thrilled that we surprised her with a cake in my office. After she blew out the candles, they urged her to "skip around the room," which, for Erica, was a challenge to not only climb on the furniture but to continue to dance for ten minutes, wearing out everyone in the room. I recently found a video of one such event, at which Carole, Julie, Brett, Jill, Tina, Andrea, Bev, Kristy, and Jean marveled at her perseverance. I also have a photo of Erica sitting on Jill's lap.

I look at the joy an adult brought to her and what she gave back. Over the next twelve years, she and Julie would form a bond. Erica often asked her, "Hey Julie, are you single?" Julie thought Erica could do no wrong. Erica deserved such fans.

Chapter 5

Alone Together

From my journal
June 30, 1988
The past fifteen months have been the most impactful in my life. Carol and I were officially divorced in January, my having left April of last year. I still have not fully come to grips with it, at least the pain. I've "thought" of the pain but have not "felt" it, except when I lie in bed at night missing Erica. I don't feel as badly anymore about leaving since I am still in her life and I feel so very good I continue to make an impact. Carol married Matt and despite my feelings, Erica has some semblance of a normal family life. I am on an MTV cruise and *Remote Control* host Ken Ober just poked his head in my cabin. I turn thirty-five one month from today. I wish I had set my life on a better course long ago, but I would not have had Erica touch my life and make it what it is.

July 10, 1988
I'm sitting at JFK on my way to L.A. I'm very angry with the new, long commute to see Erica. Erica and I had a great weekend, though. We

went on the Central Park horse ride; saw *Big Business* with Lily Tomlin and Bette Midler, had frozen hot chocolate at Serendipity, and bought a Roger Rabbit doll from F.A.O. Schwarz. Lots of politics at work, which I play well, but my focus is so much on rebuilding and being the best dad I can be.

July 26, 1988.
Back to L.A., as I did what I have been able to do, move my business to see Erica. I am deciding whether to fight the move of Erica … this divorce and separation from Erica has also been a healing process. I saw Alan again last week. My daughter is getting to know her cousins. I have started to learn how to build a new family again.

During this time, I bought Erica a Teddy Ruxpin talking bear and figured out how to make my own tape, saying things like, "Hi, Erica. It's Dad. What did you do today?" She would, of course, answer Teddy, and when she was done, she'd press his stomach again, and I would be saying, "That sounds like fun. I'm making a fancy dinner tonight," and so on. This would enable her to hear my voice any time she wanted, if she was sitting around or waking up in the middle of the night.

Book report by Erica Kluger
November 1988

"The Giraffe and the Mouse"

Once upon a time long, long ago, there was a mouse whose name was Arthur.

One day he decided to go on an adventure in the jungle. But, he met up with a giraffe whose name is Tommy.

At first he thought Tommy's legs were tall twigs, so he started to climb up them. It tickled Tommy so much that he started kicking.

Both of them got really scared that they started running around in circles.

Nobody ever saw them again………..

Until!!!!!!!!

From my journal
December 25, 1988

Christmas Eve, though we're Chanukah kids. Erica is upstairs sleeping in my new apartment (a duplex!) on the West Side. A "good Samaritan" stole my car earlier today. A great Datsun 280-ZX. Too bad I didn't take insurance. A Merry Xmas! We managed to make a joke out of it and get a good laugh. How can I get nuts when what's important is snoring upstairs? Louder than her grandmother!

October 21, 1989

Well, despite saying I was journaling, it's been ten months. Erica is watching TV. I took her to temple here in the city this morning. She loved it. I plan to take her again if she wants. It's important to have her know her faith and culture. I have felt this need to go to temple. Not hard to figure out. With Erica living in Port Jeff, Mom, Dad, and Alan in Miami, and no family here, I need to have a sense of community.

November 8, 1989 I attended my first father-daughter dance at Erica's school. She was almost seven and wanted to show me off. At that age, there was a lot more running around by the kids and less dancing, but we managed to get in a few. At thirty-six, I still danced like a fifteen-year-old and was the hit of her event. Since it was an "Erica weekend," we stayed at the Marriott WindWatch, which had an indoor pool, and we had sushi for dinner. Since I was not seriously dating then, I planned my weekends to stay on Long Island at her favorite hotel, eat her favorite bagels at Bagels N A Hole Lot More, see her favorite movies and, yes, become regulars at Splish-Splash, the aquatic water park in Riverhead. I am convinced the adults pee in the water.

Chapter 6

The Paradigm Shift: A New Start

From my journal

January 12, 1990

I had quite a date last night. This woman, Hope, is smart, very hot, and almost as funny as me. That's all I will say, but I got to tell ya …

January 18, 1990

I am in L.A. on business, thinking about a date I had last week with Hope. She "looks" like a bimbo, but she's really smart. Ha ha. I never dated anyone as beautiful as her. This one is different. But I feel like shit, run down, tired, tender lump under my arm. The doctor wants to test me for non-Hodgkin's lymphoma. Just what I need. Erica to lose her dad.

March 3, 1990

I think a lot about Hope these past six weeks. We went out on our first date on January 11. It's just so easy. She's about to meet Erica in two weeks. I don't know who's more nervous, Hope or me. Erica has only met two women the past two and a half years or so, but she goes up to women in the park and says, "Hi. My dad's single!" It's so funny and cute. She just wants me to be happy. It's better than having a dog.

March 17, 1990

St.Patrick's Day and we are sitting in the apartment. Erica met Hope this morning in the Village, and we went to The Duplex to see a kids' musical variety show of young Broadway actors. I hate Broadway kids! They called Erica on to the stage, or rather she volunteered! She and Hope walked down the street talking and laughing. There seemed to be a "plan" unfolding; these two have something else in mind.

July 8, 1990

Erica sits downstairs figuring out some New Kids on the Block routines. We're getting Hope at 11:30 then taking Erica home out to LI. I told Hope I love her in April, and it's a good relationship. Many needs, wants, satisfied. And she gets along amazingly with Erica. Erica said she loved Hope ... a few weeks before I did. Maybe she knew something I didn't yet. This feels so right. This may well be my new family.

Late summer, 1990

I am spending the weekend with Erica and Hope. I have always balanced time between Erica and my social life, but Hope is such a major part of my life—this is who we now are and Erica could not be happier. They go off and do "girl" things and bond. And they gossip and keep secrets. Erica just wants me to be happy. No Cruella De Vil here.

Barry Kluger

September 10, 1990

Holy crap. Guess who's getting married? Yep, me. I told Hope a few weeks ago that after a trip to Disneyland and Europe this past summer, I wanted to take her to Hawaii and then to Florida for Thanksgiving to spend time with my family. Hope told me if I was looking for a travel partner, look elsewhere. So, unknown to her, I shopped for a ring. If I let her go, I'd regret this for the rest of my life. We went to South Street Seaport with Erica, Glenn, Penny, and Alley. It was pouring, and I told Hope I needed to talk to her outside. It was torrential and I was getting soaked. I got down on my knee and asked her to marry me. She told me she didn't know if she heard me right but thought she'd say yes. We went back in, and Erica was jumping up and down, excited, and we told her the good news. She had a new family.

March 10, 1991

I'm married and this time, I know it will last forever. I am a better person than I was thirteen years ago. The wedding was fun. We had planned to marry in Florida, but Hope's dad had another heart attack and we thought it best we keep it in NY. We had a unique plan for the wedding. We had a ceremony in our apartment, cleaned out all the furniture, and Hope walked down the staircase from the twelfth floor to the eleventh, one of the benefits of a duplex. After the service downstairs, we all went to the roof while the caterers came in and set up. We invited seventy-five people from 1:00 to 4:00 PM, and seventy-five from 3:00 to 7:00. It worked out well. Erica had a great time, and my folks watched Erica as Hope and I went to stay at The Empire Hotel for the night. Erica beamed for two reasons: She had a new family, and I was a "happy daddy." Erica had a name for me, Ham, named after a character named Hammy from a *PeeWee Herman* HBO special. I think it was because I WAS a ham.

Chapter 7

"You from Joisey? I'm from Joisey!"

Hope and I moved in December 1992 to Montville, New Jersey. We had looked on Long Island, specifically Cold Spring Harbor, but could not find anything in our price range. It would have put me within a half hour of Erica. But the new 180-mile commute to see her was something I would do and not mind.

In New York, Erica had had a pull-out couch to sleep on. In Montville, she had her own bedroom, TV room, yard, clubhouse, and swimming pool. We could not keep her out of the water since Carol had enrolled her in a swim class when she was just three months old.

Erica was just over ten and still wanted to spend weekends with me. Her friends out in Port Jefferson were plentiful, but she quickly made new ones by us. We had a big farm next door, where Erica would go pumpkin picking. We'd go out for sushi every time she came to stay.

By this time, Erica had a new brother and sister from her mom and Matt, and it was difficult for them to have a stable nuclear family when she was spending every other weekend with me. It was no longer feasible for me to go out mid-week to have dinner with her, so every weekend was lived to its fullest.

Carol and I had our differences over the years incorporating both of our extended families into Erica's life. These issues took their toll on Erica.

One Friday night, as we were driving back to New Jersey from Long Island, Erica sat crying in the front seat. I asked what was wrong. She said, "I don't know where I belong."

I was shattered. Had I created this emotional confusion for her? I deduced that I had and resolved to do whatever was necessary to give her a sense of place.

After that, I changed my schedule to be a large part of her life during the week. This meant leaving work at 5:00 PM to attend a dance recital at 7:30 out on Long Island, stay for the final number so I could see her, get back in the car, and get home about midnight. In my mind, there was no other choice. It's what fathers do.

By spring of 1993, I had the routine down. I spoke with Erica by phone every night and was doing my best. We were settled in, and the weekends with Erica were working out, considering the circumstances.

"A Sense of Place"
by Barry Kluger

I received a fax the other day. From my daughter. From her camp. From her bunk. From her bedside.

Montville (New Jersey) is a far cry from the technology wonderland of the Silicon Valley and some years removed from the places where traditions don't die hard, they just roll over and succumb to progress. The Fourth of July celebration in my town was little changed from those I recall from my own Long Island childhood.

But the politics that were once divisive seemed to blur as I watched the parade go by with my neighbor. There we were, war protestor and Vietnam veteran, watching a bed race and seeing our own children now living in a world where the Cold War is over and the threat of attack a distant worry. Now comes the process of educating her that there is still war in Bosnia, that some governments are corrupt and hateful, and that because the immediate danger to our own daily lives is absent, now is the best time to learn and grow.

Yet, at eleven years old, my daughter, Erica, seems miraculously innocent with just a faint hint of sarcasm. A recent exchange at a local playground helped put a new perspective on these times. A seven-year-old, exhausting herself and her sisters on a teeter-totter, ran up to her mother and told her, "We're playing pretend movie theater—can we have a tape for the VCR?"

Erica has already been to more than seventy-five movies in her lifetime in a real theater (all right, so it was a ten-plex at the mall), watched planes take off and land at a local airfield, walked in the mud without shoes, and has even made Silly Putty copies of the Sunday comics. A pioneer child of the nineties? Hardly. A pure suburban kid untarnished by progress of the twentieth century? No way. Then how about a regular preteen who will remain mired in the past, watching today's hip kids forget the good old days? Not if I can help it, for this is where the lessons get passed down and she keeps it alive.

It took me eight years to get a VCR, using the excuse that my daughter's high energy level kept me from sitting uninterrupted through a rented motion picture. Truthfully, I was reluctant to give up old TV habits. And what do these confessions have to do with July Fourth? Tradition, of course! No, not the backward adherence to outdated principles of an archaic era; just a longing for those simpler days before Nintendo, Cuisinarts, Dijon mustard, digital watches, microwave ovens, and battery-powered salt-and-pepper shakers. Somehow, Ping Pong was more challenging, Gulden's on a hot dog much tastier, hour and minute hands more reliable, and food cooked in a conventional oven easier to digest.

Now, don't get me wrong. I drive a late-model import, fly only jumbo jets, wear shoes by exotic foreign designers, use an electric razor, and love automatic teller machines. So what's my point? Worried about a generation of kids who won't know how to walk to school? I was never swayed by my father's three-miles-through-the-snow routine. No, the only thing you get by walking to school in the rain is wet. No, for me, it's letting my daughter know there are movies shown outside the home, and people, not machines, build skyscrapers. That you can have just as much fun feeding ducks as shopping for designer jeans, that planting cucumber seeds in her own backyard garden rivals swapping *Melrose Place* trading cards with the kid down the block who sports the name Spike etched into his head.

I won't ask her if she thinks a) money grows on trees b) I own stock in the electric company or c) I think we live in a barn, because today, some money does grow on trees if you plant it right, people trade utilities and do own stock in the electric company and, yes, people do renovate barns and resell them for half a million dollars in the name of gentrification, ruralization, and colonization. Those particular arguments hold little water and fit nicely in that category of archaic lessons.

My wife recently remarked that I probably get my kicks going through old yearbooks, calling old girlfriends, and hoping that fringed jackets, be-ins, and rock operas all return to be in vogue. Hardly, some things should stay relegated to the sixties, seventies, and eighties. I just want to save some of those things for my offspring.

Several months ago while on business in Florida, I found myself minutes away from my parents, and I thought it would be nice to visit. My father, taking delight in grandfatherhood, asked what Erica and I do for fun. Without having a chance to answer, he ventured we probably do nineties things—computers, rollerblading, and watching the "'boob tube": all this from a man who thinks there hasn't been a good TV series since *The Fugitive*. And he's right.

Harry Chapin tells the sad tale of a boy who grows up and has a son, and then that son goes on to be like him, detached and not having the time to enjoy life.

Well, not to worry, Dad. We, like you, are stopping to smell the roses, not the phony silk flowers. For my daughter and me, it may be Newark Airport, not Idlewild; *Beauty and the Beast,* not *Godzilla;* and tossing a Frisbee, not playing S-P-U-D … but the song remains the same; the lyrics just change a bit. I spoil my daughter rotten. She has the most up-to-date Game Boy, her own color TV, and a collection of videos ranging from *The Mighty Ducks* to *The Adventures of Little Donna Karan: A Designer's Tale*. But she also takes hikes, bakes cookies, makes great lanyards in arts and crafts, and wants to be a lawyer.

Sadly, these days, the spirit of holidays like the Fourth of July and Labor Day is half-price sales; lower than low, cheaper than cheap. People pay their respects at malls.

No, this time was different. I switched off my modem and headed down to Main Street. Some of my friends insist my values are rooted in fantasy. Perhaps, but for me, reality is where I go to work each day and dreams are where I play.

I live in a world where some people still know how to have a good time. In fact, just the other day, I told Erica that if you tie a string to these two paper cups, you can talk to people in China. And you know something ... it worked.

(Published in the *New York Times,* June 14, 1993)

Chapter 8

Camp Danbee, 1994

Erica was always independent and loved to explore, so going away to camp at an early age was something that was natural for her, just like it was for me in my youth—although I went to four camps in six years. I guess I was a "bad" camper. She went to Camp Akiba for one summer, but it was at Danbee, in Hinsdale, Massachusetts, that she really started to come out of her shell—not that she was ever really in it.

June 29, 1994
Dad and Hope:
I HAVE TO TELL YOU SOMETHING!! Today at the campfire, Kendra (the head of campus) got proposed to by Eric (the head of gymnastics) and he sang her a song, and she said yes!
Well, bye!
Love, Erica
p.s. I miss you guys!!!

Barry Kluger

July 15, 1994

Dear Erica:

I can't begin to tell you how happy I was to see you on Sunday, even though it was brief.

I don't want to be corny, but … I was so impressed with the way you carry yourself, the way you took charge during the League games, the way you coached the kids, and the way all your friends seem to gravitate to you. (Gravitate: was that a Regents word??!!!)

It was a big wakeup for me in that I know you'll always be my little girl, but last Sunday, I saw a budding young adult.

I think maybe I always treated you like a grown-up, sometimes when I should have let you be more of a little child, but I always told you stuff, talked TO you, not DOWN to you, and always gave you choices.

I worried (parents always worry) if you would feel comfortable coming into your own, and I don't worry (okay … a little) much because in the camp environment, I saw someone who was sure of herself and someone I was very proud of.

You may not think it was a big deal, but it was to me. Hope made a big point of talking about it. In fact, we talked about you on the way to Boston … all two and a half hours (you probably slept when you went on your trip for the last hour!!).

Anyway, I'm so proud of what you're becoming. I saw a lot of me in you … popular, eager to help, and just all-around nice to people. The only thing different is you don't have the same facial growth I do. I guess you're a lot of people … bit of Mom, Matt, the kids, Pop-pop, Lorraine, Grandma, Grandpa, and Hope. (Just don't get the singing part from her). If this letter sounds confusing, it's just that the years have gone by so fast.

I am ALWAYS here for you to be mature, childish, secure, needy, wanting your space, or wanting a hug.

I can never replace the years not together, but I hope the times we have been together mean as much to you as they do to me. I now have an entire drawer of everything you ever made me, every card you ever sent, tapes of everything you ever recorded, and I have you to my heart every day.

Shannon and Jade and Samara seem like great kids. I like them, and it looks like you've made some special friends. Keep them. I kept mine (Ozzie, Steve, Phil). Let's figure out a date for all of you guys to come to NJ for a long weekend. Hope and I want to make sure you know your other home is in Montville, even the spooky room (ha ha).

Call Grandpa on Friday morning. I'll e-mail Jay and ask him if you could make a call. Wish Grandpa luck. This is a tough surgery, but he'll be okay. We need him to remind us of all those bad jokes. Have a great summer. Use some phone minutes for me.
I love you, Pinky.
Dad

Chapter 9

Arizona and This Thing Called the Internet

Early in 1995, my sister-in-law and brother-in-law moved to Arizona. They had read that Phoenix was one of the best places to live, so they moved to Tucson, assuming it was a suburb of Phoenix. Lori was also pregnant with twins, and, though they would be premature, with one having mild cerebral palsy and later diagnosed with Asperger's, they would grow up to be monsters, in a good way, not to mention, great, loving kids Erica would embrace over the years. Hope and I came out for MTV business in February that year for the first time and thought Arizona would be a place we wanted to live. The natural migration for Jews on the East Coast was Florida and that was not for us. But it would be four years before we put our money where our mouths were.

June of that year, I left MTV Networks to join my old colleague, Ed, at Prodigy Internet. It was a strange new world of HTML code, Web pages, and lots of people with short-sleeve shirts and PCs, though I had been on the Web since 1989. Clearly, I was no longer in show biz, but being part of senior management afforded me more flexibility to see Erica, though the drive from White Plains to Long Island was now taking four hours roundtrip. You do what you have to.

I hated the Cross-Bronx Expressway, which had been under "construction" for twenty years, and there was no getting around it. But that summer, we ended up getting a share in the Hamptons, which put me thirty minutes from Erica, and I scheduled those weekends with her around our share for June before she left for camp. I was indeed fortunate. Since Erica had grown up around adults, she was comfortable and natural around them. She was embraced by everyone who met her. We would often run into her mom and Matt and the kids at an outdoor market in Amagansett, but it was probably one of the best summers I could remember. Less time in a car, more time to bond.

From Camp Danbee
August 2, 1995
Dear Dad,
Hello. Guess what? On Tuesday, I hit my head, and it was bleeding. They checked my records to see if I needed a tetanus shot. Oh, we also have lice in our bunk. Other than that, camp's cool. Gotta go. Please write soon.
Love,
Erica

Chapter 10

It-ly, Not Italy

Erica decided to take her first-ever trip to Europe with her class in 1996, and so off she went to Italy. It was a pretty brave thing for a fourteen-year-old to do, but she was fearless. We arranged to speak by phone one day, and, when she called, I was greeted with a "Bonjour, Papa! Como esta?" Languages were not her strong suit, but I got the message loud and clear.

Much of that year was a social whirlwind for her. Our weekend visits took the form of lunches on Long Island, as her teen years were filled with boys, parties, and fun. I would leave Montville at 8:00 AM, get to her home by 9:30 (so much easier on a weekend morning), have lunch, see a movie, go for ice cream, and then head back. It was difficult not having the time I used to, but I remember my parents once asked me in 1972 to go with them on a trip to China with a teachers' group and I refused. Why would a nineteen-year-old want to travel with his parents when he could party at home? Silly, in retrospect. Erica enjoyed every vacation I took her on, until her social life got in the way.

A Life Undone

By 1997, I had no friends left from my years in Tenafly with Carol: for the most part, our mutual friends either had become hers or had simply disappeared from both of our lives. Hope and I had made new friends who became Erica's new extended family. We had tried for a few years to have children but with no luck, so Erica, for the most part, was surrounded by adults, albeit fun ones. We would have barbeques, at our home or drive into the country for the day and have dinner and do fun things. Erica rarely misbehaved. I think it was either because she was worried about coming between Hope and me or because she was afraid to be "thrown out like an old shoe," something she had said to me when she was five that had obviously come from the hurt and anger I had left behind in my previous life. I was now the guy who would buy her a pony if she wanted it.

I left Prodigy at the end of 1997, with a successful management takeover and a buyout. I decided to see if I had enough of a reputation to start my own crisis communications/PR firm in March of 1998. I started building a new professional life and a new identity. My first industry conference was coincidentally held in Phoenix. People came up to me, saw my badge for Kluger Media Group, grunted, and assumed that since I was not at a big company, I could not do anything for them. Nevertheless, I went out on my own and was successful.

Back home in Montville, one weekend in April, we entered a Father's Day race for Gay Men's Health Crisis in Manhattan, for which Hope had donated legal work over the years. Erica and I had numbered race tags and actually finished and got T-shirts. We were proud of the fact that our friends' network was made up of people with different cultures and lifestyles. I'd like to think that her acceptance of everyone was largely a result of the diversity she saw in our personal lives.

Lori and Jeff were now firmly settled in Arizona, and Erica and I went out the summer of 1998 to look at colleges and houses, since Hope and I had agreed we would move there. She would take another bar exam; I would move my PR business. Erica and I drove around every day for hours and where most kids would get bored, she was excited for two reasons: it was a new adventure, and I think she wanted to get away from what she saw as a strict household back on Long Island. We found a community in North Scottsdale. It was pretty desolate since the highways had not yet been built, but she loved it. We looked at various models, and she decided which of the rooms in it would be her room. Her plans were to finish high school in New York and then go to college in Arizona. After viewing every community the city had to offer, we decided Bellasera was the place.

We then spent a day down in Tucson visiting the University of Arizona, but Erica preferred Arizona State University in Tempe, close to where we would live. I was torn because if we chose a home, we would be moving by the end of 1999, before Erica had finished high school. I had promised her, and myself, we would not move until she finished school on Long Island, so I had trouble altering our plans. Erica thought that was stupid and that most of her senior year would be filled with parties and such, and she knew I would make plans to see her.

Hope came out to Arizona on business in October and loved what Erica and I had chosen. We planned our move, and I promised to make sure I stayed a part of her life. I was not going to abandon her.

Chapter 11

Hi Ho, Hi Ho

In November of 1998, Erica turned sixteen—"sweet" for the most part and typical for the rest. One of the rites of passage is the Sweet Sixteen party, and since Erica didn't know many people from her second home in New Jersey, I asked what she would prefer to do. She said, "We always have fun at Disney World. Let's go there." I was thrown for a loop that this was how she wanted to celebrate. No one else. No friends. Just me.

Ever since Erica was two, Carol and I had made it a point to take her to Orlando, and we had gone as often as we could, since it was a great opportunity to see my folks who lived four hours away in Boca Raton (which translates to "mouth of the rat"). We flew down and checked into a Disney World resort, of course, since I spared no expense. I think Erica knew I was at least as excited as she was to go and experience the theme parks and roller coasters. My mom was seventy-three at the time, but you could not keep her off Space Mountain. She'd been an adventurer all her life.

Erica and I had this little thing we always did when we went away: she would sleep on the edge of one bed, I would sleep on the edge of the other, and, during the night, we would reach out and grab hands to make sure the other was there—or, more important, to show that we were linked forever.

After we got back from Orlando, we went to Erica's favorite Italian restaurant. The owner, Drew, welcomed us there, and we sat and talked about the week we had just spent at Disney World. The waiter took my drink order and then looked at Erica. "And for you, ma'am?" Erica said, "I'm only sixteen," and he apologized.

Then, a look of panic spread across her face, and in that Valley Girl kind of tone, she said, "Omigod, he thinks we're on a date!"

I told him she was my daughter, and he apologized, saying he often saw older men with younger women in the restaurant and he just assumed. Once the shock had worn off, she laughed. As I looked at her sitting across from me, for the first time I noticed a *woman*. It was perhaps a bittersweet moment. But I had just returned from a Sweet Sixteen week at Disney World with my daughter, and I felt I was the luckiest dad in the world.

Hope and I flew to Arizona during Christmas week of 1998 and decided to buy a home that was different from the one Erica and I had selected. It would begin construction in early May of 1999 and be ready for us in November of that year. Despite Erica's assurance that it was okay for me to leave the East Coast before her graduation, I had my guilt about it. On the flight home, I told Hope I could not live in that model and wanted the other one. She gave in, later admitting she thought I (and Erica) had made the right choice.

The year 1999 was to be spent preparing for the move and making the transition. Most of that year was uneventful, except for the recurring problems at home with Erica and her stepdad, with Erica pushing the envelope as only she could. By the fall, the house was almost done. Hope had flown out and taken and passed the Arizona bar exam. I was assuring my clients that I was easily reachable and would continue to service them fully.

The last weekend with Erica was tough as I tried to tell myself it was okay—and, according to her, it really was. On October 26, I flew out to Arizona, having said goodbye to the moving company that morning, and left a big piece of my heart with her. The land of guns and cactus was to be our new home—and Erica's too, in just a few short months. No one could have predicted what this new life would bring.

Chapter 12

Howdy, Pardner

For our first holiday season in our new home, Erica came out to visit at Thanksgiving. We had shopped for furniture before she arrived so that when she went to her new room, it was fully furnished in a style that she had chosen. She even had her own phone line.

The year 2000 turned out to be more chaotic than we expected. Things back on Long Island were not going well, and Carol and Matt and Hope and I talked about Erica's finishing high school out in Arizona. It meant her losing a year, but Carol and Matt had been stretched to the limit, and they had a new extended family to keep together, and Erica just wanted to do as she pleased. I arranged for her to transfer to the local high school. But the mood changed from week to week, and it was finally decided she would stay and finish school in New York. During those nine months after we moved, I went back every three weeks, flying into Islip Airport just twenty minutes from her home, checking into the Marriott WindWatch, and spending as much time with Erica as her burgeoning social life would allow.

My dearest Hope,

Today, March 3, 2000, is our anniversary, and I thought I'd dispense with the store-bought cards and use my own words. Simply, I adore you, love you, and cherish you. I always wondered what a great marriage would be, but I have stopped wondering for I have it. Right there in front of me.

I watch you sleep at night. Did you know that? I look at you and smile, but no one sees me except me, your father, and G-d. Then, I go back to sleep, unafraid of scorpions. For if I get stung, love always eases pain. Remember that game as a kid— stone, paper, and scissors? Stone always won? They were wrong. Love always wins.

Nine years so far, and so many more to share. I think we all go through things in life, and we are rewarded for our patience. I waited to find you, and it was well worth the wait.

We have an exciting time ahead of us. Our lives will change with Erica. The daughter I so painfully "left" fourteen years ago will now really be a part of our lives. Imagine. We are a family. A new one, with headaches, laughing, yelling, crying. We'll adjust. You and I will communicate, and you know, in the scheme of things, we will be fine.

On this day, I say Happy Anniversary. Thank you for the love, the support, the looks, the laughs, the things that make me love you more every day, and I cherish every day I get to love you.
Barry

Barry Kluger

To: Admission for Scottsdale Community College
FR: Ira Sterne
March 10, 2000

Erica has been a joy to know and to teach. Her cheerfulness and giving nature has brightened up many a day for me. She also added to the learning environment by simply being Erica Kluger—funny, enthusiastic, caring, and friendly. I haven't met too many people in any of my careers who is quite like her, and that's a shame because we need more people like Erica.

Father's Day, 2000
Dear Dad,
I didn't have any money to get you a fancy present, but they say the best gifts come from the heart. I just want to give you my thanks. Thank you for always being a great dad. I know that you miss not being there to meet my friends, not being able to punish me, and not seeing me in my bad moods (well, maybe not the last part). I miss all of those things too, but you are always there for me. I know I don't call a lot, and it seems like I don't make an effort, but I am always thinking of you. I can't wait to come out to Arizona. Then you'll get to see my bad moods but at least we will finally be together. So, Happy Father's Day. I love you so much.
Erica
(The best girl in the world who got a 74 on her Chem. Regents exam)

Erica was preparing to graduate, which was almost not going to happen. Like me, Erica had an A in personality and a low C in her academic endeavors, but somehow she squeaked through and we flew back for her graduation and prom.

A Life Undone

The night of the prom, we went to Carol's house, and everyone seemed to get along, though it was a bit strained. But it was Erica's night, and nothing would get in the way. She looked beautiful, hanging out with all of her girlfriends whom I had met years ago but had seen little of over the years since my time with her had been spent just with her. Her date was a boy named Jimmy whom she had told in fifth grade she would go to the prom with. She kept her promise. She went off to her parties. Hope and I flew home, and I got ready for Hurricane Erica to hit Arizona two weeks later.

Chapter 13

The Long, Hot Summer

Erica arrived in Arizona shortly before July Fourth weekend and settled in nicely. I had bought her a new car, a red Honda Civic. One of the requirements was that she get a job, and I helped her put together a résumé. She'd held jobs before at a day camp and a CVS back home. She would make contributions to her phone bill, do chores around the house, and "become a human being." She was going to be attending Scottsdale Community College in the fall with the hope of transferring to Arizona State (which her best friend, Shannon,, from the Camp Danbee days, would already be attending) after one year.

That summer, however, was one of a young girl gone wild! Having a social life and a car meant bending the rules, breaking them, lying, and playing me like a fiddle.

I found that my new six-cushion couch was not only comfortable but also carried with it exclusivity reserved for fathers of daughters from first marriages who get into fights with their new spouses. One week in mid-September, as I lay watching an Arizona monsoon light up the night sky, I slept alone—not for the first time and not for the last!

After almost ten years of a blissful, fulfilling marriage, Hope and I had hit a bump in the road, as we call it, where our foundation suffered a slight tremor, not a life-altering earthquake. Four weeks earlier, Erica had moved in with us, and this was the most time I had spent with her since my divorce more than thirteen years earlier. No longer was I playing host to a toothless, cute-as-a-button, every-other-weekend little girl; now I was the new custodial parent of a nearly eighteen-year-old, rap-loving, ballet-dancing, Doc Maarten–wearing, and MTV-watching young adult.

Since the breakup of my marriage in 1987, this was the first time that the "just us" life of my wife and I had been altered, and the strain was starting to show. Caught between guilt and wanting to be a fun dad, I waffled on her curfew in her new hometown of Scottsdale, wanting to treat her like an adult, yet not wanting to let go of her as a child and not wanting to be the typical parent we all swore we would never become.

Hope had told me I refused to take a stand because I was afraid my daughter wouldn't like me. Phrases flashed through my brain: *Cruel, unfair, bitch, you don't know what it's like, how dare you judge me?* but also a more humbling one: *You are right. You hit a nerve, and I'm going to sleep in the other room because I won't admit to your clarity of the situation.*

Divorced dads carry a lot of guilt, as we all know. We are the subject of article after article, movie after movie—so we overcompensate, overindulge, overbuy, and overlove. There is some point where we "love" too much to the point of insincerity, because we want to be liked, and my wife was so on target.

She had her own issues about how my relationship with my daughter compared to her relationship with her father, but those were her issues, her demons, her memories, and her baggage. It was also her outside-the-fishbowl view that forced me to see my relationship as it really was.

> From: Hope
> To: Erica
> Subject: You
> Sent: Tuesday, September 12, 2000 4:21 PM
>
> Dad called to tell me he met Chad and "what a nice boy." I am so glad for you and want to share your happiness. I hope we can get back to that point we were at before all this stuff started. I know what it's like to be seventeen (after all, it wasn't so long ago for me!), but you also need to get some responsibility and self-discipline—that means pounding the pavement (which means spending lots of time and energy) to find a job and then keep it and going to work even when you don't want to. Self-discipline means doing things you have to do but don't want to do and WITHOUT ANYONE HAVING TO TELL YOU.
>
> You told us we treat you like a child, and you're right. And that's not something we enjoy. I'm selfish, and I'd rather laugh and have fun than have to discipline you and punish you, so you know what to do to get it back the way it was with us and with your life. Only now

you also need to be more responsible and do that SELF-DISCIPLINE thing (you'll know you're doing it when you find that you're doing things you don't necessarily want to do—like waking up with a hangover and going to work).

We want you to be able to live on your own one day, but honestly, at this point, I'm scared that you don't really have the tools, the skills to be able to fend for yourself. You need to show us (without us having to tell you) what you need to do—simply, you actually have to PROVE to us that you know how to be responsible and be self-disciplined (and, oh yeah, that includes emptying the dishwasher and the garbage).

We hope that by grounding you this month, it will make you appreciate "freedom" that much more and show you that there are consequences (and by the way, you actually did it to yourself; we just gave you consequences for YOUR actions), so the purpose of this e-mail is just to let you know that I want to go back to our relationship and make it even better. I want to be able to treat you more like a grown-up and less like a child. I can be lots of fun (as you know) so now you need to do your part to get it right!

Love,
C.D.V. (Cruella de Vil)

Since that day, thirteen years earlier, when I got out of my Honda Accord, I had always wondered *what if I hadn't left,* but I was sure it had been the right decision, albeit not the easiest.

Erica's mother, a caring, sensitive, beautiful woman, had found herself the victim of a young man who did not know what he wanted or where he was headed. But we both spent the next thirteen years reinforcing that Erica, along with a new stepfather and stepmother, was loved and that she had done nothing wrong. She was a victim of circumstance. Having been raised by her mother and stepfather, Erica had grown up in a home with rules and lots of love. Everyone did the best they could to make her feel special. I must add here that if we were all waiting for that "thank you" for the sacrifices made and the trials and tribulations lived, that phrase was still some time off, since as a forty-seven-year-old, I have only recently voiced my appreciation for a childhood and a life well lived to my own parents.

So here I sat alone on the couch, marveling at the person I now faced in Erica— a grownup of sorts, with a menstrual cycle and a license to drive.

September 25, 2000
Dad,
Well, I want to do two things in this card. The first was to, in a way, thank you for punishing me. I feel that I learned my lesson. Second, like I said to Hope, "Thank you." You have really done so much for me, and I want you to know I appreciate it. I know how I screwed up—got fired, failed two courses—but I know how to fix it.
Love,
Erica
P.S.—Can we consider/talk about my going out this weekend?

A student teacher named Stef at Erica's high school had kept tabs on how Erica was faring in Arizona and wrote her the following note.

October, 1, 2000

Erica,

So I had to threaten you to get you to write back? Bad girl! Your letter was the best entertainment I've had in a long time. I'm glad you are happy and you're enjoying AZ both personally and academically. Your man sounds nice, and I'd like a little more detail, please. What does he look like? You're not my student anymore, so I can ask for juicy details. So you missed my thirtieth birthday! I talked to C for like an hour today and I told him I heard from you. He says hi. I go up to the school every once in a while, and I get attacked and begged to come back, but I just can't. Okay, honeybunches, that's my life, sporting events and job interviews. I'm glad you are doing well in school. Keep it up because I want you at ASU soon. I was just thinking today, before the mail came, how much I miss you, ya brat! Stay out of trouble. Keep in touch and no excuses accepted.

Love & kisses,

Stef

December 29, 2000

Dear Erica,

I am writing this letter to you at 5:00 AM Apparently, if I dig into myself deeply, I am troubled by your self-indulgence, attitude, and neglect of contacting me after my call of three weeks ago. Before I continue, you are an ingrate who is lucky to have a mother and father who sincerely care about you. Also, a Gram and Gramps, a family in Miami, and your mom's entire family. Cousin Lisa came home from college yesterday, and she too called you weeks ago but no response.

Ok, Erica. Enough of the guilt trip. You appear to have alienated yourself from all who really care about you. Needless to say, I have been aware of all the problems since your arrival in Arizona and before—long earlier.

Personally, I think you are more concerned with how your `s see you, and you treat family with a "hell with all the others" attitude. Erica, stop stepping over people for your own interests. I am aware that age eighteen is a period when peers are very important. This is true and understandable. It IS possible to have room in life for friends AND family. Another troubling factor is your attitude toward me. I am aware that you view me as an "old lady to humor," and SAY what you THINK I want to hear. From years ago until today, THIS is not true. Yes, I am older, but I wanted to hear gut feelings from you, not the usual talk leading to a possible gift from Gramps and me. However, it is not easy to be objective with my own grandchild, plus I kept hearing in my own ears "she really doesn't care and doesn't really give a darn."

I could go on but see no sense. I wanted you to know that we care and we are disappointed in you. We hope you can straighten your priorities and realize all the love from us, coming and present, will never be gone. Your mom and dad are hurting.

Eri, get rid of your self-pity and start analyzing yourself. In essence—grow up!

Try to use this letter as another start between all of us—or as a finish line. I sincerely hope that you can return to a better relationship with the family plus Matt and Hope. They also care and have been hurt. Use the phone periodically without being suggested by Dad.

I love you yesterday, today, and tomorrow. I will always think of you with hopeful thoughts of the future and oodles of love.
A better New Year 2001.
Love,
Gram

Chapter 14

Prelude to a Loss

January 29, 2001

Stef,

I am so sorry that it took me so long to write back to you. So much has gone on. Well, I decided to throw myself a birthday party when my dad and Hope were in California. Sorry to say, I got caught so I got kicked out and now I am staying with my friend Shon until March 7. Then I am moving into an apartment. But things are good with my Dad now.

Tell everyone I said hi.

Love,
Erica

By March of 2001, Erica had been in Arizona for nine months. She had enrolled in school at Scottsdale Community College, gotten a job at Great Indoors, gotten fired from her job at Great Indoors but never told us and had failed a semester at SCC. Over that period of time, I had practiced "tough love" but not without feeling much guilt.

Erica then took a job at Earl's, a local bar and grill, as a hostess, and it was there that she started to experiment with drugs. The bar scene was one in which people who tended to work late would come in after a long day and blow off steam. She started experimenting with drugs in January and, within eight weeks, started to spiral downward.

During that eight-week period, she moved from one friend's apartment to another, and it killed me. Was I responsible for the downward spiral? Had I chosen Hope over Erica? Was I teaching Erica self-discipline or making her feel she had nowhere to go? It haunts me to this day.

I would see her a few times a week for dinner and to give her money, but I could not shake the feeling I had abandoned her. I suggested she live with her friends after creating the kind of havoc young adults do when given a new set of parameters, or in my guilt-ridden case, no parameters. You can find the word "sap" under the many definitions of "divorced fathers."

On March 3, Hope and I were in Telluride to celebrate our anniversary. I had been trying unsuccessfully to reach Erica for a few days and was panicking. I had even left messages for Shannon, who finally called us and said she had seen Erica the night before and "she looked bad." Erica finally called us. It was then, with Hope driving the ship, that we asked Erica if she needed help and was she willing to do what she needed to do to "get better." Erica said yes, and we caught the first flight back to Phoenix the next morning and had Erica meet us at the house.

Through our medical plan, we found a center that would meet with us. If Erica, now eighteen years old and legally an adult, wanted to go into a rehab, she had to sign herself in. After the meeting, we went straight to Banner Health Care Center in Scottsdale, a facility in a nice neighborhood, where Erica checked herself in. Whether it was comforting or not, we discovered we were not so unique: there were many young people like Erica. But she had a rare strength and level-headedness and knew she wanted to get on the right track.

I came back later that day with clothes and magazines and saw her briefly. Driving home, I sobbed. But I knew this was a step in the right direction.

Erica seemed to feel safe, and so did we. She would attend regular counseling sessions and group discussions. After six days, she was released. I wondered if it was really enough. I sat with the attending counselor and psychiatrist who told me Erica was unique. He said she was a girl who succumbed to peer pressure but was fairly well adjusted. He saw someone who had gotten caught up but was not depressed or morose or suicidal. He saw her as loving, open, and expressive. She had a support system. She had just chosen some bad friends. Shannon was one of the few of her friends who was a positive influence and kept Erica tethered to the reality of life.

After Erica came home and settled in, she was given a set of rules to follow, which included getting rid of the people who were triggers of bad behavior in her life.

House Rules, March 10, 2001

1. Clean car completely.
2. No money until a fulltime job. Pick up remaining check, and money will be taken out to pay house-phone bill, cell phone, and negative balance in your bank account.
3. No going out until you get a full-time job.

4. If you don't have enough gas, I will drive you/pick you up from work and/or therapy till you get your first paycheck.
5. Curfew on weeknights is 11:00 PM (including Sunday), 1:00 AM on Friday/Saturday.
6. Until you get your first paycheck, if you don't have gas, your friends can pick you up at the house or you can borrow from them.
7. No phone calls incoming after 9:00 PM Outgoing is fine. Pay for long-distance.
8. Cook; clean up after yourself when asked—not "in five minutes."
9. Break curfew, stay in two nights.
10. Have $1,000 in checking account before getting your own apartment.
11. Call Peter or Steven and tell him what's going on with you. NO stopping by Earl's to "see your friend."
12. You will attend therapy meetings and agree to random drug testing.

From our end, we will respect you as long as you respect us. The old tension of the past will be forgotten, and we will all start fresh in our attitudes. You have learned that the people you can trust are your family and a few select friends who are clean and have been there to help you out, not the ones who have been there to party with and then have abandoned you when you were close to the edge.

This can go rather quickly and you can be on your own, turning your life around, working, and going back to college. We will pay for college room and board, if that's the path you take, as long as you keep a part-time job. If you get an apartment in a few months, it will be a shared apartment with a roommate we agree to.

We love you and want this to work. You have so many wonderful qualities and can be anything you want to be in your life. We will help you and, if you fall, we will help pick you up if you help yourself.
Dad & Hope

Over the next four weeks, the smile came back to her face; she looked good and was exercising at the clubhouse. She was doing chores around the house, including the one I hated most, loading and emptying the dishwasher. She loved to do what we did when she was a child—doing a laundry load and taking it out of the dryer and dumping it on her because she loved the warmth of clean clothes.

Erica's Journal
March 20, 2001
Let go of what others think. Okay. Maybe what complete strangers think, but I worry about what my friends and family think. I need some sort of approval from someone in order to make a decision. I haven't stopped thinking about Chris. I have so much to say to him.

I totally understand what they mean at all the meetings when they say "one day at a time" and "just for today." I need to stop worrying so much.

March 22, 2001
Let go of the future. This is something I just recently learned at my meetings. Right now, I am focused on myself. I need to get on track and straighten things out. At first, I thought this would be hard and it still is. I'm the one who always asks "what if'" and plays out situations in my head. But I'm starting to believe in this higher power thing. Let life just take its course.

Barry Kluger

March 23, 2001

Let go of trappings. It also said to follow your heart. I want to dance and go to school. Ultimately, be successful. My fake ID is missing. Last time I saw it, it was zipped up in my bag. Now it's gone. Dad said nobody's been in my room. So much for trust and honesty!

March 24, 2001

Cultivate inner peace. It also said to be happy in the moment. That goes back to letting go of the future. I guess it means don't worry about a problem until you are faced with it. Hope finally told Dad she threw out my ID. She said it was in my car. Bullshit. I just need her to admit to it. That pisses me off.

April 4, 2001

Erica,

The past few months have been tough. I saw a supportive, loving father become a different person—one that was difficult to be, one that was necessary to be, but through it all, I never stopped loving you or wanting the best for you. You fell, YOU got back up, and I know you'll stay up. But remember, no one is as tall as when he stoops down to help someone. Let's be there for each other. I love you, and if you stumble, I'll help you get up. Happy one month clean.

Love,

Dad

A Life Undone

Erica Two Weeks Old, December 1982

Four Months, March 1983

Oskosh, 1983

A Life Undone

Road Warrior, 1984

Playing House, 1985

Barry Kluger

Snoopy, 1985

A Life Undone

Erica and Carol, 1985

Barry Kluger

Home in New Jersey, 1986

Bulding a Snowman, Winter 1987

A Life Undone

Long Island, 1987

Empire State Building, 1987

Father-Daughter Dance, 1989

A Life Undone

Outside my NYC Apartment, Summer 1990

Home in NY, 1992

Bowling for Dollars, 1993

Shooting the rapids, Vail 1994

A Life Undone

Cousin Jesse's Bar Mitzvah, 1994

With Hope at Camp Danbee, 1994

Home in Montville, 1995

A Life Undone

Passover, 1997

Sweet 16 Disney World, Just Us, 1998

Graduation, 2000

A Life Undone

Senior Prom, 2000

Erica and Shannon, Arizona 2000

Erica Winter 2001

PART 2: UNDONE

Chapter 15

A Day Unlike Any Other

I was playing golf the morning of April 6, 2001, with my childhood friend Walter, near my new home in Scottsdale, Arizona, where I had moved with Hope eighteen months earlier. I had met Walter when I was seven months old, when my mother took me across the street to see Sid and Anita's new baby. We had been friends for forty-seven years and had been the less-than-dynamic duo, getting into trouble and being totally inappropriate at the worst times.

We left the house at about 7:30 AM for an 8:20 tee-off. I thought about waking Erica so she could see Walter, but she was not working that day at Tuscany Salon up on Pinnacle Peak, so I decided to let her sleep, figuring we would see her later that day.

Shortly thereafter, Erica evidently got a call asking if she could come in that day. As it was six miles to the salon, she must have left at about 8:20. According to police reports, at 8:34 AM, where Pima Road curves sharply at Jomax, Erica drifted into the northbound lane and was

T-boned by an early-model Chrysler driven by a sixty-four-year-old woman from North Scottsdale.

On the eleventh hole, I called the house to check my messages. There was one from Scottsdale Hospital, telling me my daughter had been in a car accident. I called the hospital and asked the woman answering the phone, "How bad is it?" She replied simply, "Pretty bad."

It was 10:14 AM, and I did not know she had been dead for seventeen minutes. They don't tell you that on the phone, especially if you're getting into a car to rush to the emergency room. I threw my clubs into the car, with a few irons spilling out into the parking lot, but I didn't bother to pick them up. The 101 freeway had not yet been completed, and I drove like a madman, though it would have been prudent to let Walter take the wheel. I called Hope's office and told them to track her down.

I screeched into the parking lot twenty-eight minutes later and walked up to the desk. I was taken to a waiting room where I sat. A few minutes later, a priest walked in with a doctor, and I simply said, "She's dead, isn't she?" They nodded.

I was asked if I wanted to "see her." I declined. I wanted to remember the last time I had seen her, the day before, alive, not dead. I have not regretted that decision.

I didn't cry. While I waited for Hope to come, I called Carol and told her the news. She kept repeating, "What are you saying? I don't understand!" and I repeated the news over and over, trying to make the unthinkable believable. I don't remember much after that, but I hung up and started to think, *Where do I bury Erica?*

The next call was to my mother in Florida, who, maybe not much to my surprise, was a pillar of strength. She had lost both of her parents and was no stranger to grief. I was. I was one of the fortunate few of my friends who, at forty-seven, had parents still together and very much alive.

Hope drove into the hospital parking, jumped out, and ran up to me. I said, "Erica's dead." A guttural scream erupted from her as she grabbed me and kept sobbing, "I'm sorry. I'm sorry. I'm sorry." Her mother, Joan, and sister, Lori, followed soon after, and, when they heard the news they both broke down. For some reason I could not understand, my focus was on how I had to help them—my wife, Hope, Erica's mother, Carol, my family—get through this. There was no time for my grief, as someone had to keep this family and extended family together.

At about 2:00 PM, I got into the passenger seat of Hope's Saab, and, with Walter following in my SUV, we drove to the police station to pick up her "things." I remember looking at things through a filter, knowing Erica was indeed gone, but an eerie calm came over me. As we drove into our community, Hope told Kevin at the gatehouse that Erica had died, and he started crying. It reminded me of an old *Life* magazine photo of a man sobbing when he heard the news of the death of FDR. Kevin knew Erica as the girl who just waved as she sped through the gate several times a day, but, I would later learn, she was someone who touched many lives.

We got into the house, and I walked to Erica's room. The bed was, as usual, still unmade and the floor was littered with all the possessions one eighteen-year-old girl could possibly have. I sat there and just looked around. She was not coming back to this room … ever.

That afternoon, Hope, Walter, and Lori started making the phone calls to people here in Arizona, back East, and other places. I went into my home office and gave Walter a list of names of people to call and what to tell them.

That night was the night before Passover. This was supposed to have been special, as it would have been the first holiday Erica would spend with us since moving out to Arizona to (sometimes!) go to school. It was particularly important because Hope and Erica had experienced the usual estrangement that often happens between stepmothers and stepdaughters. The first seder was to be a reconciliation between Hope and Erica, since they had just recently settled their differences and established a good relationship. They had been looking forward to making seltzer-infused matzoh balls, which are much bigger and fluffier than those made without seltzer. This was to be their moment.

Steven and Dana, our new closest friends in Arizona, former New Yorkers, came by and gave me the name of a grief counselor at Arizona State University, Dr. Jeff McWhirter, and urged me to see him … soon. It was then I knew that I had no book, no primer, and no experience to figure out how to get through this. The decision to go the next day would be one that would save my marriage, my sanity, and my life.

The rest of the afternoon became a steady parade of friends, acquaintances, and even some strangers calling and stopping by with food. Jews believe comfort food cures everything—it's a cultural thing we have done for generations to purge our hearts and souls. Also, the holiday was beginning at sundown, and we were not making the seder as planned. With a house full of people, Hope and I walked out to the backyard, where she put her arms around me and said, "We will have a good life. It will just be different." That's who we were, who I was. The glass was always half full to me, and this was going to be the ultimate test of my character, my fiber, my threshold, my pain. The capacity for happiness is in me, always has been and always will be, and my wife will share joy with me. She has that capacity to love and nurture and spread it forth.

I spent most of the evening sitting in Erica's room, smelling her hand lotion and her perfume and looking through albums. I was numb enough to fall asleep, but Hope told me I was sobbing well into the morning.

April 6, 2001 4:56PM
To: Plainview Reunionites
FR: Steve Cohen

I have some very bad news to deliver to all of you. I just received word that Barry Kluger's daughter, Erica, was killed in a car accident this morning. She had been living with Barry and Hope in Phoenix and was on her way to work when she had the accident.

As it turns out, Walter Osband happened to be in Phoenix for work and was visiting with Barry today when Barry got the call about the accident. Walter called me to tell me.

I just spoke with Barry. He asked me to relay the news to all his friends from Plainview. He is taking calls, although he still is in shock over the news.

Like all of us, I always relied on our dear friend, Barry, to handle the broadcast of news to the Plainview group.

A few months ago, Barry brought us all together to share in the warmth and comfort that only old friends can bring to each other. Barry now brings us together again, to share the pain of his loss and to give him the comfort that only old friends can bring him. I know that if Barry

was writing this message, he would end by saying, "Tonight, hug your kids before you go to sleep."
Steve

That night, as I walked around the house, I went into the library, looking for nothing in particular, and came across Richard Nixon's book *In the Arena*. In it I found a quote I had highlighted years earlier but whose full impact I had not felt until that moment. "Greatness comes not when things always go good [sic] for you, but the greatness comes when you are really tested, when you take some knocks, when sadness comes. Because only if you have been in the deepest valley, can you ever know how magnificent it is to be on the highest mountain." This from Richard Nixon, of all people! Go figure!

Chapter 16

The Morning After

Saturday, April 7, we headed down to Tempe to meet with Jeff McWhirter, the grief counselor. I didn't know what to expect or what to say. I assumed it would just flow, and flow it did. The hour-long session remains a blur, but over the next twelve months, clarity arrived. I had been a good father, perhaps not a great one, but I had done the best I could.

Later that morning, I went to Starbucks with my friend Steven and ran into a person who two hours earlier had called me with his condolences. Now, he was with a different crowd and stood up to hug me. When the embrace ended, Steven and I walked to my car. I turned to look back and saw them huddling and shaking their heads. And then I realized ... *I* was the topic of their whispered conversation.

I never knew what it would be like to be the one people point to and say, in hushed tones, "He's the one who lost his daughter."

Quite often we project looks of sadness onto other people, either to help us feel special in that we are getting attention or because we want to believe the world is grieving as we are.

I had spoken to my brother, Alan, and he had told me he was getting the family together, my mom, sister-in-law, and niece and nephew and would be in Scottsdale on Monday. Because Erica's death had fallen on a Jewish holiday, we could not bury her until early the next week, Tuesday, April 10, to be exact.

When Hope heard my brother was not immediately getting on a plane, she called him. I learned later that she made it clear he was to be in Arizona the next day.

Saturday morning, Hope's mom and Walter went to look at caskets, something I could not and would not do.

I had reached the point where I was now saying to myself, "Twenty-four hours ago, Erica was still alive. Thirty-six hours ago, Erica was still alive." Simple to understand. We want to go back in time, like in the *Superman* movie when the Man of Steel reverses the earth's orbit to bring history back to the moment before Lois Lane is killed in a landslide. I guess that only happens in the movies, not real life.

I spent some time on the phone with Carol. Always a rebel, Erica had gone through a period of estrangement with her mom and Matt, but they had finally made their peace. Their original plan had been to come out to Arizona that weekend for a family reunion of sorts. The plans were still in place, but now they were coming out for a funeral. To this day, I will never understand how Carol found the strength to make that flight.

Earlier, we had agreed Erica would be buried in Arizona, her adopted home. I could not put her in a box and send her back east in the cargo hold of a plane. Fifteen feet above, people would be drinking, laughing, and watching in-flight movies, while just below them would be stillness and silence.

That night, the house was filled with dozens of people, but we did not follow strict Jewish tradition. There were no cardboard boxes to sit on, no soft shoes, and no covering of the mirrors, which is done so you don't see the face of grief in your reflection. But I was not about to become a super Jew overnight. I knew God would understand.

Chapter 17

Passover and Palm Sunday: Faiths Converge

TO: Barry
FR: Abbie (a former employee)
Dear Barry,
When I heard the news about Erica, I was devastated. Words cannot express my deepest sympathies that go out to you and just want you to know that you are in my thoughts.

I didn't know Erica, in fact I never met her, but I sure felt like I knew her through the experiences you had with her that you shared with us and the anecdotes you brought to the office. Whenever you mentioned Erica, you always spoke with pride and a gleam in your eye. You could tell you had great joy in being Erica's father—even during the challenging times—and she sure was lucky to have you as a dad. During these very difficult times that lie ahead, hold on to those great memories of Erica that you will have forever.

I'm happy that you and Hope have a deep love and respect for each other that will help during this difficult period.

I'm thinking of you.
Love,
Abbie

Sunday, April 8, Hope and I went to look at Paradise Memorial Gardens, and when I saw the mausoleum, it had a sweet smell of lavender that turned my stomach. I could not put her there, but I could not bear the thought of putting her in the ground. I had been afraid of cemeteries since the summer of 1968 when a group of us at Camp Pocono Ridge snuck out and went to an old graveyard across the way.

Something about this place was different. There was a lake and no headstones, just plaques and memorials in the ground. It looked more like a park than a cemetery, and I thought Erica would like the view of the McDowell Mountains. Somehow, that mattered. We met with the woman who handled such things and was relieved she didn't look like the undertaker Mr. Graves in the TV show *The Munsters*. This was all so normal in a world of chaos.

My brother, Alan, arrived early Sunday afternoon. When he got out of the car, he hugged me in a way he had never done before, and his strength fused into me, something I knew I would be able to rely upon. It seemed that my dad was too ill to travel, his having been on dialysis. But there was more: Dad was angry, real angry, at God. He had called his rabbi in Florida and let loose a tirade as to what kind of Supreme Being takes a child, a daughter, a niece, a grandchild. My dad had been the first Kluger to live past fifty, his own father having died of a heart attack at forty-seven. His life had had some downs but mostly ups, and this was unthinkable.

My father had always been known as Funny Lenny, the guy who always had a joke and a smile. His life had been particularly good. He was a warm man but not one who verbalized his feelings. We spoke on the phone about Erica. When he hung up, he said, "I love you." Oh, how boys need to hear their dads utter such words! It was a sign-off he would continue to use on the phone with me until the day he died.

Erica's best friend, Shannon, had always been the "level-headed one." She was Louise to Erica's Thelma, behind the wheel, steering the excitement. (Erica had spent most of her time at Shannon's sorority house and, I would find out later, the frat house of her first real boyfriend, Chad.) Erica and Shannon had been inseparable. Shannon could not make sense of her death. Even today, she wears a shirt of Erica's when she goes on casting calls in Los Angeles and gets strength from her memory. She even "sees" or "feels" Erica from time to time.

The calls flooded in from around the country and from friends overseas. People were saying things like "God had a plan," or "She's in a better place." I was not angry, knowing their words came from the heart, from personal grief, or spiritual belief. Sometimes the words gave solace, sometimes they elicited anger, but the amazing thing was that they brought out emotions … and feeling something is what all of us in grieving want. We want the tears, we want the floodgates of sadness to open and then be damned up by remembrance and strength.

Meryl from California became a mainstay during my grieving process and well beyond. She didn't fly, and, although she did not attend the funeral, she was there in so many ways. Although she was fortunate enough not to have experienced my pain, somehow she really knew me and was always beside me.

My friend Ira put it to me this way: "If God had given you a choice between 'a wonderful little girl named Erica, full of life, whom you will never get to meet' or 'this jewel that you will get to know but only for eighteen years,' which would you have chosen?" Maybe that's what belief and spirituality are all about—believing that we are given options, and, while they may not always turn out as we expect, we can reap some wonderful and joyous years.

They say life is for the living. Death comes when life ends. I say life ends when we can't see the beauty in everyday life, in our spouses, partners, in our jobs, in our family, or in memories.

Just a few weeks before she died, Erica asked me why six was afraid of seven. I told her I didn't know. She said it was "because seven ate (eight) nine." She was a kid not only in age but in heart. I found myself looking forward to life. I was not afraid of seven. I was not afraid of anything. For with my wife, Hope, and Erica in my heart and soul, somehow I was on top of the world ... for a while. It would not stay that way.

I went down to the Sinai Mortuary with Hope to meet the owner. He said I had to do it. Not for legal purposes, but for a reality check and closure. Closure? Who was he kidding?

April 9, 2001
TO: Barry
FR: Brett (my former assistant)
I will always remember Erica as a beautiful little girl who would play in the office, and we would go get lunch for the department and draw pictures together. I couldn't help but laugh when she would say, "Brett, you have to play with me or my dad will fire you!"

She was you, and in a way, you her, full of laughs and joy.

Barry Kluger

She was so loved.

While I dealt with my grief in Arizona, back home, Erica's friends were experiencing the loss of someone close, most of them for the first time. Erica's friend Jenna spread the news.

Subject: Erica Alexis
Date: April 8, 2001
From: Jenna Nelson

Hi, Everyone,

It's kind of hard for me to write this, because I never thought I would have to. I have to write some things about my best friend. I moved to Ward Melville High School in tenth grade wondering who my new friends would be. I don't exactly remember how I met Erica, but now I remember why I can never forget her. She always looked to the brightest side of things—to her the glass was always half full. She befriended everyone who came through her path. Whether you were a teacher, coworker, acquaintance, janitor, or complete stranger, Erica wanted to be your friend. At Stroud School of Dance, she helped teach children how to dance, which was one of her passions. She loved children and became close with many of them as she worked as a summer counselor at The Laurel Hill Day Camp.

I think about all the fun times we had with her, like pool hopping at night in the town of Poquot or hanging at that beach. One of the fondest memories I have with Erica would be a day when we walked along the shoreline from her beach in Old Field to West Meadow Beach with Holly and Katie. It was a gorgeous day, and we shared so many laughs. Or the many afternoons spent on the benches at Sea Port Deli drinking an iced tea that she herself had gone behind the counter and made. She loved Nick Carter from the Backstreet Boys and thought he might marry her. Erica was bubbly, energetic, and kind to all who crossed her path. Each and every one of us can remember the many times that she was there for us and was able to lift our spirits.

When we found out she was really going to move to Arizona to live with her dad, we were equally upset. We didn't want to lose a true friend for life, because that is what Erica was. The morning she was going to move, a few of our close friends surprised her at the airport to bid her goodbye. We all cried with her and hugged her. In January, I went to visit her in AZ. I will tell you that it was one of the best times of my life. I was so happy to see her when she greeted me off the plane. I can remember exactly what she was wearing that day—a long green frilly sweater. It fit her personality perfectly. We had so much fun that week that I didn't want to leave. I made plans with her to move out there and get a place with her.

I spoke with her this past week for about an hour just trying to catch up. She told me that she was going to come home in June because she knew everyone would be home for the summer and she wanted to see all of you. Her family from Long Island was coming out to visit her the next week in Arizona, and she was excited to see them.

If you knew Erica as well as I did, then you know that she wouldn't want any of us to be upset. She would hope that maybe we all could take a little something from her personality. Whether it is her generosity, kindness, strong will, or humor, you decide. I will never forget the footprints she has left on my heart.
Love,
Jenna

Chapter 18

A New Week

From my journal
April 9, 2001

It's Monday, April 9, and tomorrow is the funeral. Today would be a full house, with everyone flying in, but first, there are some things we had to do. After a morning visit with Dr. McWhirter, Hope and I had to stop by the tow yard to get what remained in her car. Books, magazines, most of her room! Hope went in the office and told me to wait. About ten minutes later, she came running from the back lot, crying, telling me NOT to go look at the car. She told me later no one could have walked away from the wreck.

My mom, sister-in-law Amy, Jesse, Lisa, and an unbelievable outpouring of friends descended upon us. Surprisingly, most of my friends are women (go figure), and Jill, Mindy, Robin, and Marcie have arrived from points east and west. Ira is in from New Jersey; Glenn from California; Bo from New York; and my new best friend, Gary, from Miami.

Carol, Matt, Alley, and Zach came in the night before and went to the funeral home to see Erica one last time. I could not go. I would not go.

According to Aish.com:

Jews call death "the crisis of life." How a person handles death indicates a great deal about how he or she approaches life. As there is a Jewish way of life, there is a Jewish way of death.

"As he came, so shall he go," says Ecclesiastes. Just as a newborn child is immediately washed and enters this world clean and pure, so he who departs this world must be cleansed and made pure through the religious ritual called *taharah*, "purification."

The *taharah* is performed by the Chevra Kadisha (The Burial Society), consisting of Jews who are knowledgeable in the area of traditional duties, and can display proper respect for the deceased. It therefore demands that all Jews be buried in the same type of garment—a simple white shroud. Wealthy or poor, all are equal before God, and that which determines their reward is not what they wear, but what they are. The clothes to be worn should be appropriate for one who is shortly to stand in judgment before God Almighty. Therefore, they should be simple, handmade, perfectly clean, and white. These shrouds symbolize purity, simplicity, and dignity.

Erica was pure in so many ways. She saw good in everyone, and it was fitting that her burial ritual reflected her innocence.

Carol's side of the family, with whom I had maintained a good relationship, was there. After all, the love we had for Erica was our common bond. Whatever had gone down over the years had no place in this house of mourning. We forgot the fights, the disagreements, the jockeying. The funeral would be the last time I saw Carol for nearly seven years.

By now an avid cigar-smoker, I sat in the backyard with friends and family, and somehow humor came through from me. I had certainly been changed forever, but I did not become a different kind of person. No anger, no "Why me?"

Hope started a new practice that weekend where she would just scratch my back as a way to calm me and connect. It still gives me comfort.

I went through Erica's stuff to find things to put in the casket. I chose her pager, which she was never without, one of her favorite stuffed animals, a New York Port Authority bridge token (we would play this game on the two-hour drive to visit on weekends where she had to guess which bridge or tunnel I was thinking of), and a CD. I think it was one by Eminem, though I was not a fan. I once asked her why she liked this guy who referred to women as bitches and hos. She had replied, "Dad, I listen to the beat, not the words." That made sense. My parents felt the same way about Led Zeppelin, and, to this day, I can't tell you what a "bustle in your hedgerow" is. I gave it all to Steve to bring to the funeral home.

There was food all over the place. The lifelong Jewish tradition was intact. When things were bad, people would say, "Eat something; you'll feel better." There was a modest amount of truth in that. I excused myself, went into my room, and started to pick out a tie for my suit.

Chapter 19

The Show

The phrase "the show" has several meanings, but in baseball it refers to the major leagues. It doesn't get any higher than that, and this was the ultimate. It was April 10, and I was getting ready to bury Erica.

TO: Barry
FR: Peter
Sent: Tuesday, April 10, 2001 2:44 PM

Dear Barry,

The news of your loss has hit me very hard ... I had a difficult time sleeping last night. Barry, I'm not the best at keeping up my share of communications, so I hope you know that I love you, respect you tremendously, and care a lot about you.

You would have never thought back in high school how difficult life is. I've lost my brother, and both kids have serious medical problems.

Yet we must always try to count our blessings, our family, friends, and loved ones, which you have so many of.

I know I am not expressing myself well; I want you to know that I am thinking about you, and I love you. I will speak with you soon.
Love,
Your old Marilyn Blvd (not to mention Binnewater) pal, Peter.

My brother-in-law, Jeff, and Lori arrived to drive Hope and me to the temple so that Carol and I could meet with the rabbi. We went into his study together. Earlier that morning, I had thought I was handling it all so well. Someone had suggested I take a Valium. The doctor's office never returned my call about getting a prescription, so I got on the phone and uncharacteristically started yelling at the receptionist, "I'm going off to bury my daughter! And I need this!" Of course, they got right on it. It was clear the veneer was starting to crack.

Jeff and I joked in the car about some trivial stuff, and when we pulled up to the cemetery, I thought I was in the wrong place. There had to be more than two hundred people there, and we had lived in Scottsdale for only eighteen months. Erica had been there less than a year, but all the kids she had met in her brief residency were at the service. At Arizona funerals people wear short-sleeved shirts and are pretty casual. This was an oddly beautiful day. The sun was shining. Fitting perhaps because her all-too-brief life had certainly been a celebration. On headstones, they say the dash (–) between years is the most important part. It's what happens during that span that identifies a life—identifies a person and how he or she lived.

As we got out of the car, we saw the hearse. I remember Glenn, Ira, Neal, and a few others went to the back and got ready for their role as pallbearers. I felt as though I was watching someone else's life, but I also had an eerie sense of clarity.

I sat with Hope, Carol, and other family members under a tent while the crowd overflowed onto other plots. I looked up and noticed a few faces I was excited to see. Josh and Dina, Randi and Jeffrey, Mike and Adrienne, and many people I hadn't expected to see: If there was ever a moment when you take note of all you have done and all your children have done to leave a mark on other people's lives, this was that defining moment.

Rabbi Ken Segel was head of what I called the "rabbinical Mafia" of Arizona. He was head of the oldest congregation in Phoenix and though he was thought inaccessible, the man I came to know over the next few months and years helped guide me through this morass of emotions, including anger at God. He spoke, and was choked up. Losing a child, we have heard so many times, is not normal. His eulogy was wonderful.

Erica's stepfather, Matt, spoke, reflecting a family that was full of love and sometimes conflict, which we all had. I still wonder if Erica was the catalyst or the divider, until I realized she never asked to be a child torn between two families and two lives. This was not what she had bargained for.

Next, Erica's best friend, Shannon, spoke. Poised, beautiful, and mature, she was nevertheless a young woman who didn't understand that death can come at such an early age. When you are eighteen, you are supposed to live forever. You are not supposed to die. Not this way.

Then it was my turn. I had spent the entire previous day writing out what I wanted to say. Writing had always come easily to me, and eulogizing my daughter, while unfathomable, had come just as surely.

Barry Kluger

My words had been written in a time of great grief but full of great love. I had not taken the Valium—it was still in my pocket.

As is traditional, we, the immediate family members, went right home after the burial, which I think is a stupid practice. You want to move among the crowd, kiss people, cry with them, laugh with them, recognize them, and thank them for coming. Instead, we drove home from the cemetery to get ready for the people who would be coming by to mourn with us.

Chapter 20

Shiva

From Aish.com:

Shiva ("shi-vah" or seven) is the weeklong period of grief for the seven first-degree relatives: Father, Mother, Son, Daughter, Brother, Sister, or Spouse.

Grandparent or Grandchildren are not included. As most regular activity is interrupted, the process of following the shiva ritual is referred to as "sitting shiva."

Shiver is the more appropriate word for when your entire body shakes but some unknown force inside keeps you from totally falling apart.

The house quickly filled up with people. Hope remembered the day as cold and rainy. For some reason, I remember it as having included a bit of sunshine. Obviously, I saw things very differently than did the others who were there.

More than the course of the day, over a hundred people came and went, each time washing their hands at the entrance to the house, a ritual to cleanse after returning from the cemetery. According the tradition, one washes the hands three times to signify life.

From Aish.com:

People don't always know how to properly pay a shiva call. Talking about death makes people nervous and awkward, so the house often turns into a festive gathering filled with nervous chatter instead of the proper house of mourning.

One who has come to comfort a mourner should not greet the mourners. In fact, it is best to come in silently and sit down close to them. Take your cue from the mourners. If they feel like speaking, let them indicate it to you by speaking first. Then you can talk to them, but what about? Let them lead, and talk about what they want to talk about. It is best to speak about the one who has passed away, and if you have any stories or memories to share with the mourner, this is the time to do so. Out of nervousness, we often babble on about nonsense because we do not know what to say.

Often, the best thing to say is nothing. A shiva call can sometimes be completely silent. If the mourners do not feel like talking at that time, so be it. Your goal is not to get them to talk; it is to comfort them. Your presence alone is doing that. By sitting there silently, you are saying more than words can. You are saying: "I am here for you. I feel your pain. There are no words."

And sometimes there aren't. Here are examples of things not to say:

"How are you?" (They're not so good.)

"I know how you feel." (No you don't. Each person feels a unique loss.)

"At least she lived a long life." (Longer would have been better.)

"It's good that you have other children," or, "Don't worry, you'll have more." (The loss of a child, no matter what age, is completely devastating.)

"Let's talk about happy things." (Maybe later.)

In our short time in Arizona, there are business associates, new friends, old friends, family, and even a few of Erica's friends, people I had never met. Baskets of food arrived all day, comfort food for the grieving Jewish soul. The day would end with the ritual recitation of the Mourner's Kaddish, organized and assembled by my friends Larry and Bud. Larry would ensure we properly respected Erica for the entire period.

Chapter 21

Shiva Part Deux: Five Days without Erica

From my journal

Wednesday and Thursday, April 11 and 12 are the last two days of shiva, abbreviated because of the holy week of Passover. For me, it means one thing: the house will be eerily empty, except for my mom who has decided to stay the week. The crowd remains strong, and it keeps me strong, for the time being. Hope will be going back to work tomorrow for a part of the day and I will be on my own. I urged her to get a routine back in her routine, which was the only way to stay sane amidst insanity.

April 14, 2001
Barry,
Thanks for sending me your beautiful eulogy. I can't quite bring myself to reread it yet, but I will, and probably many times over. I remember thinking as I listened to you on Tuesday that you had really captured her spirit and vitality, her love, her goodness, cuteness, charm, enthusiasm,

and oh so many more things that will come to mind as I continue to reflect on the times she spent with me—quality times, as we called them. I was also reminded of a very lovely article written by you and printed in the *New York Times* many years ago which captured Erica's hither-dither ways even at a very early age. I believe I still have it. I can't help but think that she was always trying to squeeze as much as she could into every day, almost as if she knew time was short.

She was my first grandchild, even before Marvin and I married, and I knew she was to be my special grandchild. Someone said to me that the terms of love between a grandparent and grandchild are unconditional. I have certainly found that to be true. My memories of her will always begin with her arms wrapped around my neck from the minute she walked in the door and until she left. I too will continue to think of her, talk about her, and reminisce, for that will keep her with me always.

I am glad to see you find some comfort in writing your thoughts. I too have always found it easier to write what I find difficult to express orally. All of us will need all the support and love and friendship we can muster in the long weeks, months, and years ahead. I will be thinking of you and Hope and am as close as the phone. When it gets a bit easier to talk, I hope we shall do just that.
Lorraine

From my journal

April 20, 2001

Friday began a three-month ritual of going out to eat whenever we can, partly to be out with friends but mostly to not be home. Jewish tradition typically requires that you not go out or observe holidays or celebrate for a year, but I was not to become an observant Jew overnight, and besides, it didn't work for me. We went to temple Friday night for services with Steve and Dana and then off to Sushi on Shea. Shellfish on the Sabbath was probably double detention, but we forged ahead. Saturday was more food: Chompie's Deli with our neighbors Dennis and Diane and dinner at Razz with Lori, Jeff, Joan, Shannon, and her dad, Steve, who had flown in to be with Shannon, who had lost her best friend.

It is one week since the funeral, and we decided to go to a support group of people who have lost children called The Compassionate Friends. It was held in a church in Paradise Valley, and when we walked in, I saw all these sad faces. Most of them were wearing photo pins of their children, some who were gone as little as four days and some as many as twenty-two years. They had died in different ways: murder, illness, or car accidents. The room smelled like death, hopelessness. I spoke and said why I was there and who I lost. As the people around the room spoke, I leaned into Hope and said, "I mean no disrespect, but these people are stuck. They are immobilized by their loss, and this is not for me." Everyone grieves in their own way, but since I could not see myself five, ten, twenty years from then carrying this pain and only socializing with people who understood my pain, we left. I would not go back.

My read on The Compassionate Friends was harsh and unforgiving, but I didn't see it that way at the time. Over the next few years, the group included Erica in their list of anniversaries of when children died. I sometimes ran into people for whom this organization was a saving grace, and for them I am grateful that the group exists.

Another organization I was told about, Alive Alone, is solely for parents who have lost their *only* child. I became involved through their newsletter. It was "safer" that way. The newsletter carried poems, memories, and stories of strength. I always told myself that one day I would attend their annual conference, which, in many ways, is a celebration. I still have not. Perhaps this book will be the catalyst.

More dining out, more grief counselor meetings, barbeques and easing into a new routine. A childless one.

Chapter 22

Florida Calls

On April 25, I went to Florida to visit my folks and to see my dad, who had not come to the funeral due to his poor health. I hosted a dinner with Mindy and Jimmy, Gary, my folks, my niece and nephew, and Ira and Amy, who were in from New Jersey on vacation. I sat with my dad, who watched so much TV that it seemed like the remote was attached to his hand, and we talked about Erica. This was the first time I remember him ever baring his soul and his pain. He was pissed at God, and he had told his rabbi that.

My dad's health slowly got worse after that visit, and he would live only another four years. I can't help believing that the death of his granddaughter started to kill him.

I was more concerned about Hope being by herself back in Arizona than about myself, but she made a few visits to Dr. McWhirter, saw some friends, and got into the *new* normal.

I returned home to Arizona four days later, and Hope picked me up. I had returned from helping my parents heal, but when would I find time to help myself?

In the weeks that followed, I got back to business. I flew out to Minneapolis on a Wednesday, was back on Thursday, and, two weeks later, drove to Las Vegas. My college roommate, Charlie, was now running a popular music and theater venue outside Chicago but had a corporate apartment on the Las Vegas Strip. Back in 1974, he had been my only contemporary who had lost a brother, coincidentally named Barry. As housemates, I was amazed at the humor and love of life he had, but even more amazed at his parents who were genuinely happy people despite having lost a child. This twenty-four-hour Vegas turnaround was to hang out, have some laughs, and harmlessly flirt and to get a primer on losing a loved one. Losing Erica had been my first experience of losing someone close to me. I had been fortunate until then. Charlie's pain was part of his fabric. I wanted to learn from him. We went to breakfast with his parents and his sister, Dee Dee, and from these people, who had lost a son and a brother, I learned about "life after death." It would be rich again, someday, I just didn't know when.

One week after that, I was off to L.A. to see friends who had known Erica. I was not running away but rather running toward continued memories and talks about her. I had always been someone who talked about his feelings, and this openness was par for the course. I had changed, but I did not become a person I didn't recognize. For the first time in my life, I really knew what I was feeling.

It was now six weeks since Erica had died, and Hope and I went to see Dr. McWhirter. Hope and I had been fighting for a week now, with me jumping at everything she said—or did. There was nothing she could do right. She comforted me at night and checked on me during the day. One evening, she couldn't reach me and came home and called for me. The first place she looked was the swimming pool, not to see if I was swimming, but rather to see if I had killed myself. I was in the front room, looking at albums and sobbing. It felt good to cry. It usually does.

At McWhirter's office, I did what I often do: imagine life, my life, as a movie. This is always something poetic and safe to do because it frames what you are thinking. I knew why I was fighting. I told her I imagined myself as Don Corleone at the end of the really bad film *Godfather III*, in which, like King Lear, Corleone dies alone, broken, full of pain, bewilderment, and loneliness. I told Hope I had pushed her away the past three weeks because I loved Erica and Erica had died. If I loved Hope, then it meant Hope would die, so if I sent her away, I wouldn't have to bear the loss of her. Cosmic, I know, but it made sense to me and to the doctor and to her.

May 15, 2001
Dear Barry,
The last time I actually spoke to you on the phone I remember hanging up and thinking to myself how great you have been in trying to hold all of us up and wondering what was holding you together. Last night after "speaking" to you, I wound up thinking that reality was finally rearing its ugly head and that you were having a tough time of it. I couldn't and wouldn't expect anything else.

The loss of Erica from the lives of those of us who loved her so deeply is something we shall *never* recover from. But you have a very "special" ability to look at memories and smile about things that were absolutely maddening at the time they were happening—like emptying the dishwasher. I found myself doing many of those same things when Marvin died—and heaven knows he didn't do too many maddening things, did he! Yet those are the things of memory and what sustains us and keeps people alive in our hearts. So smiling and a sense of humor in our grief is a good thing. And it does keep us going. The alternative is complete and utter depression and inability to function. I remember at one time someone applying that same principle to the success of a marriage.

I don't know how your grief counseling is going, but I am glad you and Hope are working on it together. I don't know that anyone can offer us anything to make it go away, but talking certainly is palliative—at least I believe that. Others talk about time healing. Time mitigates, but also doesn't take it away. I just wanted you to know that I think you have done a lot of the right things, and I appreciate your keeping in touch and being supportive. I hope I can also give some of that to you. I loved her deeply and get some comfort in the belief that those feelings were reciprocal. I also know that she loved you deeply.

I hope I have properly said the things I wanted to share with you. Give my regards to Hope.
Love,
Lorraine

Barry and Hope,
Thank you so much for breakfast this morning; I had a wonderful time as always. You two are a lot of fun and very interesting to talk to. You both look great and seem to be doing well. How beautiful is Erica in that picture! It's my personal favorite, really captivates her personality with The Delta Sig boys with her. Ha-ha. Boy-crazy Erica—gotta love her. I think you guys need a pet, just a suggestion. All right, I'm going to run and practice my lines for my scene. Stay well, and I will speak to you soon.
Love,
Shannon

Later that month, I finally went through the process of going through Erica's things and giving some things away. It had been barely eight weeks, but it was time to organize life after Erica. We had a pool table that Erica and I used to play on when she came home from work. I decided to give it away. I kept some clothes, ones that were easily identifiable with her and took her strawberry hand lotion and used it to put on my feet, less for the dryness of Arizona skin than for the scent that reminded me of her. Her room was pretty much as she had left it, though cleaned up. A pair of her ballet shoes sat on top of the dresser, next to a Father's Day mural she had made for me several years earlier.

Chapter 23

The S—List

July 10, 2001

Dear Marc (Linda and Marc, close NY friends),

I got your call. Erica died more than three months ago and we spoke shortly after.

To say that you got caught up with things is an insult to me and to her memory.

This is not a case of "Barry broke his leg. Let's see how he's doing," and it falls in the cracks. This is the most devastating thing that can happen to ANYONE, and shame on you for every time you thought "I wonder how they are doing" and did NOT pick up the phone to see. This was not about your busy schedule ... it was about us.

We considered you friends; you had met Erica many times, we even went away, and we expected more. Not a whole lot, but some concern. We all have busy lives. Mine and Hope's are a lot emptier, and for you to

not call us for so long and let time slip away is wrong. As far as making plans, I'm focusing my time on being with Hope and remembering my daughter and trying to find happiness amidst all this. I have little time for anything else that doesn't involve that, and that includes you both.
Barry

July 10, 2001
To: 'barrykluger@barrykluger.com
Subject: How dare me

How dare I after twenty years still fault those who never reached out to me at the time of my sister's death. How dare I still remember those who drifted away as the weeks passed, but my grief grew. How dare me, because now I am guilty of the same, but worse, I am forty years old, when I had no room for excuses from mere seventeen-year-olds.

Barry, there is no decent excuse, there is no asking for forgiveness, there is only the admitted recognition that I have committed a terrible act against two people whom I have grown to love, and I certainly haven't done justice to the memory of Erica.

I will go home tonight as I always do and think about how lucky I am to be so busy due to a full life. I will go home tonight and feel ashamed that I can't find the time to reach out to friends whose life is emptier without the presence of their child.

I am sick, sick over how I acted, especially when I know better, especially when I hated "those people" who now include me. Do I ask for you and Hope to forgive what I have done, do I ask you and Hope to forget what I have done, or do I just ask myself why I wasn't a better friend?

I know the answer, and it is a question for me to ask myself, and for only me to answer. I am sorry for the hurt I caused you, and I am sorry for not being a better friend.

With all the love in my heart,
Linda

July 11, 2001
Dear Linda and Marc,
What can I say? Your eloquence floored me, not because you're not eloquent, but I wish I was as connected to my feelings as you are surrounding your sister's death. I am finally coming out of my "haze" and accepting that this dying thing is bullshit. There is no reason, it's not fair, it sucks, and it's shitty.

That said, it has opened me up to move on, and Hope and I are doing well. I won't say much more because I'll wait till I see you in a few weeks. But your words, thoughts, and even your self-flagellation (okay ... I'll wait while you go to a dictionary) mean a lot. Just stop beating yourself up. We never know how to react when these things happen. We expect parents to die, not sisters ... or daughters.

Let's forget this forgiveness stuff. Just be our friends.
Barry

Chapter 24

The Endless Summer

It was now a little more than three months since Erica's death, and the summer of 2001 was in full swing. On July 19, Steve, who had been there twenty-four hours after Erica's death, came out for a few days. I was pretty ornery, sarcastic, and belligerent. Forget what I said two months earlier about being in touch.

On one of the days, Steve came to me and said, "You know, I'm a pretty grounded guy, but ... um ... last night I felt Erica in her room while she was sleeping." It gave me comfort, but I wondered why she had not revealed herself to me. I said, "Maybe she wasn't ready." Steve replied, "Maybe *you're* not."

Three days later, I was on a plane to Napa where my brother, Alan, and I were meeting for a bonding-over-golf-and-wine weekend. I remember playing really bad golf. But, for the first time, we had a real come-to-Moses moment. We laughed a lot and cried a little. At the Coppola vineyards, there was a crowd of people milling about, and I launched into a routine, asking people where they were from: I would then name the capital of their state, showing off that geography had been my best subject in school. A year later, Alan would find himself at a urinal at a Miami Heat game, and the guy next to him said, "Hey, I know you. Your brother told me my state capital last year in Napa." It always pays to listen to the teacher.

On July 30, I turned forty-eight—my first birthday without Erica. She had always made a card or bought one that she edited to say what she really wanted to say.

My folks sent me an e-mail:

We checked out some of the store-bought cards, but the meaningful were very few. So we decided to write one ourselves. We know this is a very difficult time for you, we feel your ups and down. We love you.

> When told we had another boy
>
> Our hearts were filled with so much joy
>
> Even though you were funny lookin'
>
> We saw so much potential a-cookin.
>
> You were the cleverest, loving little guy,
>
> At age two, your witticisms made all sigh—Oh My!
>
> As you matured, we would kvell
>
> Even though at times, we did yell
>
> You progressed from movie mogul to other stuff
>
> Okay. So rearing you was sometimes tough.

> You are a son, a husband and a dad,
>
> You will always be one, whether happy or sad
>
> Remember your love and Erica's smile
>
> It'll keep you alive and after a while
>
> The strength you gain back will reflect how you miss her,
>
> You'll long to give her hugs, to hold her and kiss her
>
> To you our son, we wish you much love
>
> And the smiles from the past will come down from above.

The Barry Kluger "I'm Doing Fine" tour's next stop was New York three days later for the twentieth anniversary of MTV, where I had worked for a decade and where Erica was just as well known as the CEO. She had been raised on doses of backstage access and getting "slimed" at the Nick Studios in Florida. It was the first time I had seen people since Erica's death, and it was personal for most of the people there. I had my happy face on, but it wasn't that difficult. I was among friends who had known her from the time she was four until I left the company in 1995, when Erica was a young woman of thirteen. Hope joined me a few days later in New York, and we made the rounds of well-wishers who had not come out for the funeral.

They talk about different stages of grief. Shock, denial, pain, and then anger. The anger clearly set in a few months after her death, and I was now clearing out my address book. What had been six hundred acquaintances were whittled down to two hundred—to those friends and even some strangers who had reached out. I spared no one my wrath, and I was pretty brutal. I felt it was my right. I no longer accepted the excuses that people made, such as that they couldn't call because they didn't know what to say or they thought I needed time. I needed people to not abandon me at a time when I most needed support. Intellectually, I know that such a tragedy is hard for people to deal with, but, emotionally, I took no prisoners. Hope and I were spending time together and with friends, and I had choices to make … and I made them.

I spoke to my friend Roger who had lost his brother a few earlier to brain cancer. I asked him, "When do I start to feel alive again?" He said, "Anywhere from five minutes to five years." I replied, "I don't have that much time to put my life on pause."

FR: Barry Kluger
July 12, 2001
TO: Andie and Scott

It's been three months since we have heard from you. Life is too short. The first correspondence I got was a baby announcement. We are taking you out of our address book and out of our lives.

July 12, 2001
Barry: We are shocked at your message. We were afraid to ask anything more because it seemed too painful for you to talk about it. We did not want to sound maudlin in asking questions that we knew were difficult to answer.

We always were there to listen—we thought that's what you wanted. It is difficult for us to understand your anger at us. We wanted to let you mourn, and then we would speak with you. Erica was a beautiful child. We called J and L and reminisced about the holiday that you all were here. They thought she was beautiful and fun—somewhat shy—we didn't forget about you, Hope, or Erica. It was not an obligatory ask—we were genuinely interested.

We share your pain, anger, and all your emotions. We have thought of you for two weeks—talked about it, cried about it, and tried to decide what we would say to you when we called. Your message has blown us out of the water. We are sorry that our lives are important to us. We sent you a birth announcement—after much agonizing about that as well—we also sent a donation in Erica's memory.

Barry, we have not forgotten you, Hope, or the memory of Erica—perhaps we don't deal well with these things. We wanted to be with you—our timing stank. We even talked about coming out to see you—but I suppose that is moot.

Our love to you both—we still value our friendship and the many times we shared.
Andie

It would be two years until I picked up the phone to call them, but by then, my feelings for them had waned. I just wanted to close some of the doors still left open. There were still some left to be shut, but I obviously didn't care enough to attend to them.

Chapter 25

The Veil behind the Unveiling

By mid-August, I squeezed in another one-day turnaround to Minneapolis and got ready for my parents' and nephew Jesse's visit to Arizona. My mom had not been back since the funeral, and my Dad had not seen where Erica lay buried. We went to temple that Friday night, which had been my practice for about four months straight. I felt comfortable there. Just sitting.

From Aish.com:

The service is called "unveiling" because in America the tombstone is covered with a cloth which is removed by the family during the ceremony. There is no religious obligation to hold an unveiling ceremony, but the ritual became popular toward the end of the nineteenth century in America and Western Europe and has become an accepted and meaningful practice. In addition to dedicating the grave monument, the unveiling gives those in mourning an opportunity to commemorate the deceased. It usually happens twelve months after the death.

I knew that my parents planned to come in this month, so I bucked tradition and held the unveiling less than five months after Erica's passing. I had chosen a headstone that said "You will dance in our hearts forever." Rabbi Segel did the ceremony, and we had Hope's family, my parents, and Erica's friends there. I didn't know if there were rules regarding playing music at an unveiling, but I wanted to. Rabbi Segel nodded with a "whatever soothes your soul." I turned on the CD boom box and we sat silent to the strains of Carole King's "Now and Forever."

There was now a marker displaying the dates of Erica's short life. It brought an odd sense of solace. People could walk by while visiting others or simply looking for a place of solitude, look at the dates, see this was a child, and think of her, even if they didn't know her. I put a bag of Skittles on the headstone. I used to make her give me the red ones to make sure they were "safe to eat." They were her favorites.

Proving once again that food comforts the Jewish soul, we all went to Chompie's.

August 26, 2001
B & H,
Hi, it's Shannon. Thank you so much for breakfast this morning! It was great to see all of you again. I spent the whole day in tears though—I guess the whole ceremony just brought me back to the time of the funeral. The night before, we spent the whole time remembering Erica and talking about her and laughing. As a matter of fact, we talk about her every day. I'm supposed to "get my teeth fixed and lose my Long Island accent"—say the agents—before I meet with anyone.

Anyway, same goes for you about getting together—if you ever feel like hanging out with some of Erica's "girls" and talking about her, we're

always here. I put your name and cell number on my emergency card for movement class—in case I get hurt (unlikely)—I hope you don't mind. I gotta go to bed. I'm exhausted! Talk to you soon!
Love,
Shannon

August 26, 2001
Shannon,
Thanks to you and Brianna for coming this morning and for joining us for breakfast. I think it was nice and special that your boyfriend, Chris, came too. You could have easily taken a cab to come, but for him to be with you at this time shows how special he is.

One of the lousy things when your child comes from a divorced family is that you don't get to know their friends, especially when they live far away as Erica and I did in Long Island and New Jersey.

That's why meeting you, getting to know you, and knowing how much you and Erica meant to each other gives me a little glimpse inside her life as an adult that I never would have had if she did not move here, stay friends with you, and have some of the life experiences she had—good and bad—that's what makes us what we are.

This is a weird time for parents of someone who died because they want to hang on to connections, but we know all too well that Erica's friends were her friends, not ours.

You have a full, great life ahead of you with friends and parents who love you, and I know you will cherish all of that. We have no illusions about your keeping in touch, but if you choose to say hi now and then, we would welcome it.

Barry Kluger

If it gets nuts at the sorority house, and you need a break at a really nice house with a great pool, a fully stocked refrigerator, or even need some advice from an older J97 (yeah … Hope was on her way to being that with Erica), give us a ring. We are actually quite cool … LOL.

Be well and be the kind of person that you are that I know Erica admired and was grateful for. And if you need to talk and have it kept only among Hope and me, we're good for that too. Think of us as your "get out of jail free" card.

Take care.

Barry

Chapter 26

The Dog Days of Summer

The heat was finally breaking in September. We had plans to go on a cruise to the Middle East, but something went horribly wrong: September 11, 2001. Hope was out running when one of the law firm partners, Don, called me to tell me to turn on the TV. Until then, there were two lives, one after April 6 and now, one after 9/11. I wondered what Erica would have thought. With no planes flying and a trip cancelled, we decided to drive to Telluride, Colorado, where we had been earlier that year, when I had gotten the call from Shannon about Erica in crisis. Telluride had what Hope often called "feng shui." It felt like a natural place to be for us. Bike riding, hiking and, of course, more eating. I do think Erica would have loved this place.

In late October, Shannon's folks came to town. Steve and Eileen had been wonderful in the prior six months. A week later, October 25, would be the first "celebration" we would attend—the bat mitzvah of the daughter of my friend, Jill, and her husband, Alan, in Washington, DC. It was also an opportunity to see old college friends, Maxine,

Joanie, and Rob and talk about old times, including the time they had come to New York twelve years earlier, and we had gone to a raucous diner in the West Side called Lucy's and six-year-old Erica had danced on the table.

That Saturday, we filled the temple with everyone else, and it was going to be a test for me. During the Mourner's Kaddish (prayer for the dead), the rabbi asked people who had lost loved ones to stand up and state the name of the person being mourned. I stood and felt all eyes focus on me. I summoned up enough strength to proudly say "Erica Kluger," and my friends Jill and Robin looked at me with immense love, not pity.

We flew back that Sunday. Monday morning, I had scheduled a colonoscopy and even wrote about it in the *Arizona Republic*. With death and illness around me, I decided to get a head-to-toe checkup. I didn't want any surprises. As usual, we went to eat, and I got a triple-decker corned beef and pastrami, a rare treat for me as I was getting older, not out of concern for my health but rather for my waistline.

Chapter 27

Up, Up and Away and a New Year Dawns

Lori and Jeff had given Hope and me a hot-air balloon ride as a gift, and we had planned it for the morning of November 18, just after my parents celebrated their fifty-fourth anniversary. When we got to the balloon, I refused to get in. I sent Hope on her way alone. I was still in that mood of refusing to do anything I didn't want to do. Erica's death was an excuse in many ways for avoiding unpleasant things or else just a convenient cop-out to explain my bad behavior. Hope landed safely.

November 27 would have been Erica's nineteenth birthday. Hope took the day off and went to the cemetery. Hope felt the cemetery housed Erica's body, not her spirit. I felt Erica was everywhere. I had distinguished myself for the previous months by showing up with an eight iron and chipping golf balls near the gravesite while I talked to Erica. They never bothered to tell me to stop. Shannon joined us that day.

The week of December 4, Hope went to New York on business. This was the first time she had left me alone since Erica died. I saw friends, spent some time alone, and did not, as Hope feared, jump in the pool.

Later that month, we went back to Telluride, this time to ski. It was even more beautiful than I had remembered, and I wondered *Am I getting back to "normal"?* We looked for Tom Cruise at Sofio's, his favorite Mexican restaurant, but he was not there. Hope had to settle for just me.

December 31 was the end of quite a year. We decided to have a New Year's Eve party at our house and reflect on what had transpired. It was then I decided to embrace the phrase "moving forward," not "moving on." I could continue my life and bring her with me.

I remember when we were kids and would see our friends on New Year's Eve, we would think it was funny to say "see you next year" since it was less than one day till we'd be playing again, but it was a NEW year … out with the old, in with the new. Not necessarily for me.

Then the dreams started:

A gang came to my apartment in New York with the big roof deck. They wanted to beat me up but I told the gang leader about Erica. He was moved. As they went to kill everyone, I hid under the deck. They pulled me out and chopped my head off. I watched it roll away and then I flew away with Erica, who was a little girl.

The first weekend of the New Year, we went to see our friend Peter Noone perform at the Chandler Center for the Arts. We had been friends since the VH1 days in 1992, and I knew his family. Peter and I had spoken over the months. He went into a corner with Hope, and they talked for a while. He came back and said, "Why don't you come out on tour with us for a month or so, to hang out and get a change." I thought that sounded great. Hope nodded: "Go!" but I never took him up on his offer.

A few weeks later, January 12, to be exact, Hope noted in her datebook, "Stayed home, Barry didn't feel well." That day, a Sunday, when stores are usually closed and there's a lull in the hustle and bustle, gave me time to think. There was little to distract me. For a few years after that, I stop driving on Sundays, and chose to be a passenger so I could just think … and mourn.

The next week, I was off to Minnesota to work on the closing of a company that had been a client of mine, which was shutting down after fifty-two years. I was remarkably focused. In this case, 9,500 people were losing their jobs. I had lost one child.

I was getting into a new groove and was moving forward. We were taking our first cruise on a real luxury yacht, the *Seabourn Legend* in February. I knew we would be meeting people who didn't know of my loss and who would ask the inevitable, "Do you have any kids" and I would say, "Yes. She died last year in a car accident." I would never see most of these people again. It was an opportunity to talk about her and continue my exodus from sorrow.

We went to Costa Rica, Panama, Belize, and Honduras, ending up in Fort Lauderdale. I had gone rafting on the trip and was amazed at not only how my mother-in-law acted as ringleader but also at how much I enjoyed myself. Was it too soon to laugh, knowing Erica would not get to experience this … or anything?

In Fort Lauderdale, we saw my friend Gary. My folks came to the hotel, and we went to dinner. We headed back to Arizona the next day.

Chapter 28

In Like a Lion

In March, we had our nephews, Aidan and Cutler, stay with us for a weekend, the first time we'd had them since Erica's passing. I loved kids, but I didn't necessarily want to be around them. On one hand, there was comfort in the fact that the twins had known her, but there was also comfort in seeing people who didn't.

Steve came in again for a few days, and we went to see Crosby, Stills, Nash, and Young at the America West (now US Airways) Arena, a rarity since Neil Young didn't normally tour with them—ever. As we did with every concert, we left before the end, which reminded me of when Alan and I were kids and my dad would leave the Westbury Drive-In before the end of the movie so we wouldn't get caught in the traffic.

It was the end of March and the beginning of April, and I knew what that meant.

Friday night, April 5, we went to temple for the one-year anniversary. I was invited, as I had been many times before, to sit on the *bimah* with the rabbi. As was the practice, we went for sushi afterwards.

The next day, Saturday, April 6, marked one year since Erica had died. We went to the cemetery. I was amazed at how much the grass had grown in, and angry at the same time. I wasn't sure how to mark the day, so I did what I thought was best—had a barbeque, invited our best friends, the Weinbergs, and surrounded myself with friends. It was a glorious day.

More than a year earlier, I had befriended Larry, a New Yorker who was a few years older than me. He had been battling cancer for several years, but you wouldn't have known it from his joy of life. I would see him every morning at A.J.'s Supermarket where the guys would have coffee. They ranged in age from forty-eight (I was the youngest) to a spry guy of ninety-two. I called them the Prostate Posse. One day, after learning Larry had died, his widow, Ingrid, came by for brunch. She asked me, "When does it get easier?" I told her, "Hell, if I know."

This anniversary month was one in which we stepped up our travel, going back once again to New York. I had decided to attend a big cable television event in New York, and this was to be the first time I would see many people since Erica died. It was here that I realized the people I knew through business were real people underneath their titles, and that experience restored my faith in people—not that I had ever really lost it.

That weekend, we went to see Walter and his family in Westchester, the first time I had seen him since Erica's passing. He was happy with his three boys and seemed to be powerfully involved with his kids and wife. I knew he would be a good dad but couldn't help feeling that his having been with me a year earlier had helped him know how to really savor the moments.

It was now a little more than a year since I had started seeing Dr. McWhirter, and I was growing stronger every day. I had started from a position of strength to begin with, so this was a healthy, ongoing process of growth.

Hope and I were going out to see movies more often, making plans every weekend, and, of course, going out to eat. I started going out for Wednesday Boys' (and Girls') Night at Morton's, and Hope started spending more time at Nieman Marcus.

At the end of May, we drove to Laguna to visit our friends John and David from the cruise. We enjoyed being at the ocean. A photo taken that weekend shows Hope and me on the beach, steps away from the Ritz Carlton, and we look happy and in love. We were.

"Moving On:

In the Words of Parents Who Lost Kids"
By Jeffrey Zasow

When people ask Barry Kluger of Scottsdale, Ariz., if he has any children, he replies, "Yes, I have a daughter. She died in a car accident last year. She was eighteen."

His word choice startles people, he says, but it's deliberate. He won't say he "had" a daughter. "I have a daughter. Erica still lives in my heart."

Reggie Peppers of Houston keeps a photo of his daughter, Morgan, on his office desk. In the picture, she's two years old, her age in 2000, the year she died choking on a grape. Whenever passersby notice the photo, Mr. Peppers has to explain her death. It's painful for him, but he says removing the photo would be "cheating her memory."

Thomas Meehan of Carteret, N.J., always wears a photo of his twenty-six-year-old daughter, Colleen, on his belt. She died on Sept. 11 in the World Trade Center. Because "no words exist" to describe his anguish, he says, he displays her smiling face as "a silent way to make people aware of our loss."

Last week, this column focused on the language of grief—and how there is no word to describe parents who have lost children. In response, these three dads, and 256 other bereaved parents, wrote to share their thoughts about how our culture talks about death. In heartbreaking e-mails, they told of words that buoy them, and words best left unsaid.

Dads wrote of how they'll struggle on Father's Day, hoping friends offer a few kind words. Mr. Kluger lost his only child, but on Sunday, "I'll still be a father."

Many bereaved parents wish people would acknowledge their loss with a simple, "I'm sorry." Last year, Alexandra Smallberger of Blue Bell, Pa., gave birth to a stillborn daughter. Many of her coworkers never said a word about it. On her computer, she displays the baby's footprints in a frame. "Only one person has commented on it," she says.

Janice Schacter's son died during delivery. "He never took a breath, so most people don't consider him a child," she says. But because he was Jewish, he was named and circumcised before burial. "Am I supposed to pretend that a child in his grave doesn't exist?" Ms. Schacter asks.

Trudy Pierallini's twenty-six-year-old son died last year in a motorcycle accident. She says most of her friends now avoid her and her husband.

"They think we're contagious. Just when we need them the most, they're gone, too."

Many parents told horror stories about insensitive comments. Rosita Kintz of Lansing, Mich., lost a child to leukemia and two children to cystic fibrosis. A friend, trying to explain why so much tragedy visited one person, said: "In a former life, you must have been one of the people who nailed Jesus to the cross." After Jacquelin Payne's six-year-old son drowned, a relative said to her: "It's just as well. He might have gone bad when he grew up."

As grieving parents struggle to talk about their children, others often respond with oblivious disregard. Lisa Austin of Dillon, Colo., was recently interviewed by a career counselor. Asked how many children she has, Ms. Austin said, "Three. One is thirteen, one is eleven, and one is in heaven." The career counselor replied, "So you have two."

"If people could visually see our wounds, they'd see we've been opened from neck to pelvis, with all our insides hanging out," says Ms. Austin.

Other parents also wrote of feeling "mutilated." "Part of us has been amputated," says Ted d'Afflisio of Lincroft, N.J., whose eighteen-year-old daughter, Michaela, died in March. "We continue to function, but the stump will always be there."

Bereaved parents call themselves members of a non-exclusive club that no one wants to join. They refer to parents who haven't lost children as "The Clueless" or "civilians."

Pegeen Stocus of Madison, N.J., has two living children. A daughter drowned at age two in the backyard pool. "The question, 'How many children do you have?' is a huge bomb," she says. When she hesitates in answering, some people respond, "Come on, it's not a hard question!" "Well it is," she says, "and always will be. I have a friend who lost his seventeen-year-old son in a car accident. When people push for details about his children, he says his son is a sophomore at Villanova University, the saddest lie I've ever heard."

Dave Pellegrin of Honolulu at first struggled with the big question, but has found a response that feels right. "I say, 'I have two sons. My first son was killed in a motorcycle accident.' Then I tell them about my surviving son, so people can choose which son they want to talk about."

These parents have given great thought to the limitations of language. Several said they don't like when society says they "lost" their children. Their children aren't misplaced, missing, or bewildered—the dictionary definitions for "lost."

Addie Chan of Boise, Idaho, had three miscarriages and one stillbirth, all girls. When people tell her that her daughters "walk with God," she responds. "I'd prefer if they could walk with me."

What words do these parents long to hear? Louie Silva, whose twenty-year-old son, Beau, died in March of a staph infection, has appreciated when people say things like: "Beau really had an impact on my life."

Parents wish others would share memories of their late children. "One woman said she wouldn't say my daughter's name because she didn't want to remind me and make me cry," says Maureen Carlson of Homewood, Ill., whose eight-year-old died after a horse-riding accident. "I told her, 'You can't remind me of someone I'll never forget.'"

Many grieving parents meet through the support organization The Compassionate Friends, which expects 1,500 people at its national conference in July in Salt Lake City. They'll attend eight to four workshops designed to help them through their grief. But there will be no semantic solutions.

"We're not looking for words," says David Brand, whose four-year-old son died in January. "We just want our kids back."

Published in the *Wall Street Journal,* June 13, 2002
(Copyright 2002, Dow Jones & Company, Inc.—Reprinted with Permission)

Chapter 29

Summertime Blues 2002

I went to see Dr. McWhirter before he left for the summer of 2002 (that's when the crazy people run around town with no one to talk to), and I was unusually depressed. It was very unlike me. I couldn't shake this sadness which, to date, was always there but never so overwhelming that I found joy in very little. He asked how I was doing, noting it had been "quite a year." I told him, "Well, I helped my parents, Hope, Erica's friends, and everyone get through this rough period." He asked, "What about you?" I said, "What about me? I'm fine." But clearly I wasn't. He asked if I ever thought about taking an antidepressant. I told him that was for unhappy housewives and nuts. He told me that was not true and that I had carried an unbelievable burden for more than a year. I decided to give it a try.

A few weeks later, I decided to buy myself a Jaguar. I don't know if it was a midife crisis, a reward for myself, or just a desire to get rid of the car I'd had when Erica was still alive. That next day, we went to look for dogs, since someone had said, at the funeral no less, that I "needed" a dog. We didn't get one—not this time.

The summer morphed into fall, and we decided to end November with a trip to Miami to see my family for Thanksgiving, flying down on November 27, which would have been Erica's twentieth birthday. She had died at eighteen, and now she would have been twenty. In my mind, two years had passed.

We spent the long weekend and flew to St. Thomas to start a seven-day cruise on the *SeaDream*, with John and David. We flew back through Miami and saw family once again. Life was back to "normal."

This was also the point at which I started writing a weekly column for the *Arizona Republic*. Writing was my passion and is something I continue to do to this day.

"New Road Map Needed After Death of Child"
by Barry Kluger

I don't hate Scottsdale. I should, but I don't. I hate the roads, and I hate the speed. But I love the place I call home.

Someone took my road map last year on April 6, coincidentally the day my daughter Erica died in a car accident on Pima Road. This was also the day that my compass, both moral and philosophical, was no longer useful to her and one that I am working to make applicable to my new existence without her.

In any journey in life, we use our children to define and chart our own course, looking at jobs, college, dating, marriage, children, sickness, health, tragedy, and triumph as things to look forward to, things to dread, things to ponder, all part of the lifecycle, as we have come to call it.

Immediately after Erica's death, I started to deal not only with my own loss but to figure out how my relationship with my wife, Hope, would grow, stall, expand or implode, reading a statistic that 80 percent of marriages fail within five years after the death of a child.

Marriages following any tragedy are put under a tremendous amount of pressure, and it takes two very unique individuals to find their way, determine their purpose, and execute the course of action for the remainder of their days. What I discovered was with such life events removed, it's important to make your own "markers" to replace the ones that were taken.

You and your partner become the new cartographers, the new Rand-McNallys of your own destiny, creating new roads and signposts, incorporating the cherished memories of a life now gone with a new world, of new ways, new ideas, new paths, and new dreams.

People say, "You can fall out of love with a partner, but you never fall out of love with your child." You never do, but if you allow a tragedy to compromise your love with someone who has stood by you in good and bad, there become two deaths in your life, one avoidable, the other not.

The emotions run the gamut in the aftermath of a huge loss for which we are never prepared. No one has written the definitive guide on how to handle it, as it is different for everyone. Sadly, the only way to understand is to live it, and we members of this "club" pray that no one should ever have to experience it.

But as long as we do, we can create our own new markers of which we can really chart our own journeys. For us, it is making new events to look forward to, to celebrate that which we do have and commemorate that which we have lost. There is a choice between living your life and living out your life.

Some people are born with an ability to make choices in their life, and some have choices thrust upon them. What one does with that choice, that fate, determines their character, their resolve, their commitment to live their life. It isn't easy. But we owe it to those we loved—to remember them—not recall them and, along with the people we do have, strive to make a difference with the love we have left.

Erica would have been twenty on Wednesday. I don't hate Scottsdale. It's where my daughter came to live and, regrettably, to die. Every day, I have the pain of her absence, the strength of her memory, the love of my wife and a life ahead of me. I am home.

Published in the *Arizona Republic,* December 2, 2002

Since Hope is a big skier, we went back to Telluride in mid-December. This had become a place where I felt happy and safe. We ended 2002 as we had the year before, with another New Year's Eve party at our house. Judging by the photos, it didn't look like anyone had a good time. We vowed never to have another party. That would not last.

Chapter 30

Dimming of the Light

By 2003, I no longer thought in terms of hours, day, weeks or months—only years. Since time had passed so quickly and I resumed living, though I never really stopped, the challenge was how to keep Erica's memory alive. The fund at the Stroud School of Dance that Erica had attended on Long Island was being looked after by Carol. The Erica Kluger Fund at Temple Beth Israel had been distributed among various programs since we had left the congregation. We left because Rabbi Segel did. He had been the lynchpin that had kept me there, and while the new rabbi seemed like a totally nice person, I had no connection to him.

"Am I a Father? Yes, Forever"
by Barry Kluger

"And a Happy Father's Day to all of our dads flying with us today on Southwest Airlines." I wondered out loud to my wife on that Father's Day, 2001, on a trip to Las Vegas, if I was still a father, and she assured me I was, that you never stop. But that past April, Erica's life was cut too short in a car accident here in Arizona. That Father's Day was my first since her death, and my first thought was to "get out of Dodge," avoiding the IHOPs and brunches where throngs of dads go. But this day, I thought: *There's no one to call me on Sunday.*

I imagined I would always be a father, and that I would use every opportunity to parent, maybe not my child but someone else's, through being the kind of person I am. Dads like us love, nurture, and never stop being what we are. We are fathers.

That day in April 2001, I joined a club. It's very select. They don't have dues. They don't have a clubhouse. They don't have a secret handshake. They don't have a membership card. But the cost to join is high, and while everyone can afford it, no one wants to be inducted.

It's 2003, and my third Father's Day is upon me. I struggle to find my way back to "normal," whatever that means. And while the people mean well, they say stupid things like "she's in a better place." Well, if it's such a great place, then that's where you should go when you are eighty, not eighteen.

We know what to do when we lose a job. We know what to do when we have a flat tire. We know what to do when see someone in trouble. We don't know what to do when we lose a child. Nothing prepares us for what we have to do, or feel. Sometimes, we don't feel at all, and we feel bad when we don't cry. And when we do cry, we feel it's not enough.

Three Father's Days later, there are still a lot of things I don't understand. I don't understand a lot of the things I am feeling, or not feeling. But I do know I miss Erica.

I loved her more than I can ever say. They say a father's love for his daughter cannot be described in words … I cannot find the words. The love is in my smile when I will think of her, in my tears when I think of her, in my laugh when I think of her. I will forget when the dishwasher is not emptied and wonder why Erica forgot to do it, and then I will stop and remember why. And give anything to have her back.

And for the rest of my life, I will have to make sense of this jumble of emotions.

When we are young, we know all the answers. When we get older, we know all the questions; we just don't have all the answers. I wish I knew the answer to *why?*

I will remember Erica forever, and I ask that you do the same for all the Ericas of dads out there today. To the dads for whom the pain will always be there: don't let people tell you it will take time. We should not let time heal all wounds. We have all been wounded, hurt and saddened, and if we let time heal, we will forget these people—and that is something we must never do.

I ask of all of you reading this column for Father's Day to do all us dads a favor. Walk down the hall and hug your kids goodnight, or if they are away at school or living on their own, pick up the phone and tell them you love them. We need to know that. If you know a dad who lost a child, call and tell him you know Sunday will be a difficult day, but you were thinking of him. We need to hear that. And if you are out and about, stop and give a moment's recollection of our child who is gone. Believe me, wherever we are, we dads will feel that.

And for all those dads out there who wonder if this day is still ours, it is and will always be. Happy Father's Day.

Published in the *Arizona Republic*, June 14, 2003

Chapter 31

Halfway to Being an Orphan

At two o'clock in the morning on May 25, 2005, my brother, Alan, called me to tell me that our dad, who had been in and out of the hospital for kidney failure and general body breakdown, had died. I sighed and called the airlines to arrange a flight. I was more concerned about my mother than I was about losing my dad. We had had a good relationship, but I had come to accept death, like birth, as part of the lifecycle.

We arrived late the next afternoon and went directly to see my mom, who was in surprisingly good shape, considering. We made arrangements for the funeral, and I contacted their friends. I always thought it was funny that, starting with my bar mitzvah in 1966, my mother had always kept a written list of who had given me what, and I knew it was her way of seeing who her friends were! She had made such a list for my dad, noting those who she said "gave a damn" and those who didn't. I made the calls, along with my brother, and got ready for the "show."

A Life Undone

The night before the funeral, Hope suggested I invite my mom to stay with us at the hotel. "She should not be alone." We picked her up and brought her back with us. We all went to dinner and had a few drinks. Then we got into our PJs and had a good old-fashioned sleepover. We laughed a lot that night.

The next day, there was an overflow crowd of people at the funeral home. Many were from my brother's law firm, but there were also friends he and Amy had made over the years. Also there were Sam and Terry, Reggie, Harriett and Harold, Justin, and numerous extended family members.

I listened to my nieces and nephews speak, and then it was my turn. Writing and expressing myself had always come easy, and, as I had done with my own loss of Erica, I wanted to make sure my folks' friends and families felt good about having had my dad grace their lives. I began with "A rabbi and a priest walk into a bar."

That was typical Lenny Kluger. I had them rolling in the aisles, and it was intentional. I wanted them to laugh, remember, and reflect. Alan spoke next, offering a heartfelt timeline and legacy of my dad. Alan had been closer to my dad than I had been. After he finished, he sat next to me and said, "That's the last time I ever follow you!"

Later that year, around Thanksgiving, my mom came out to Arizona and we threw a big party for friends and their parents so that my mother could have a support system when she would come to visit in the future—or eventually move out here. She was a hit, walking around in her sunglasses (inside!) and going out for a smoke. She was eighty!

"A Birthday Gift of Life for Someone Else's Child"
by Barry Kluger

My daughter, Erica, would have turned twenty-four on November 27, but she was killed in 2001 on the roads of Scottsdale.

I am scratching my head what to give her for her birthday this year, a symbolic gesture I always make. And then I thought. The gift of life. Somebody else's. With the help of Arizonans.

Arizona has a graduated driver's license (GDL) statute that two years ago the Insurance Institute for Highway Safety rated as "poor."

In 2005, Arizona Rep. Lucy Mason proposed a tougher GDL law. The bill died after concerns that it would limit parents' rights to determine when their children can drive. Luckily, Mason was reelected last week, and hopefully she'll try again.

In Arizona, a child who is fifteen years and seven months old can obtain a permit. Illinois issues permits at fifteen. But that's where the similarities end.

In Arizona, the permit holder most take driver's education or twenty-five hours of parent-supervised driving, of which five hours must be at night. In Illinois, Drivers Ed is mandatory, plus it also requires fifty hours of driving with a parent, ten of those at night.

In Arizona, after five months, there are no restrictions, other than local curfews. In Illinois, there are restrictions on passengers during the first six months, with only one passenger under the age of twenty, except for siblings and/or your own children or stepchildren, seatbelt usage is mandatory, and cell phone usage is not permitted. And next year, all permit holders under eighteen must maintain a consistent school-attendance record.

Apparently, a teenager's life is more valuable in Illinois than in Arizona, and obviously the people of Illinois love their kids more than the people and the legislature of Arizona do.

It's time to put on the brakes. Many of today's parents prefer friendship to discipline. They don't have the time, or won't find the time, to teach their kids how to drive and tell them how dangerous it is, until tragedy strikes them or someone they know. Then, of course, it's too late.

We have a citizenry in Arizona that just voted to end smoking in bars. Maybe in the coming year, our Legislature and all parents can focus on stopping the littering of dead bodies on our highways and forever changing the lives of thousands of Arizonans, their neighbors, their friends, their families.

I slow down now when I round the curve at Pima and Jomax Roads. I think of Erica, but I keep my eyes on the road. I never know what inexperienced kid is heading toward me in the opposite direction, talking on a cell phone, with no real understanding of the one-ton missile powered up beneath them.

Published in the *Arizona Republic,* Nov. 18, 2006

Chapter 32

A Pack of Marlboros and an Outstretched Hand

By early 2006, it was clear my mother was getting restless. She had come out to visit several times and loved it. I wanted her out here, since my work life gave me the freedom to spend time with her. She always had a great sense of direction and would have no trouble getting around in a new place. On each visit, we would visit apartments, condos, and upscale senior homes, where she would walk in and, not being a wallflower, get to know everyone within five minutes.

My mother-in-law, Joan, had been living in Arizona since 2000 and, though they were six years apart in age, they had a lot in common. One difference was that my mother was not interested in dating, whereas Joan was still raring to go. I always admired Joan for her social "skills." Joan was charming and sensual and liked men.

The last place we went to look at for my mom was a place called Sierra Pointe in Scottsdale. It was a great place, full of activities, vibrant people and, as my mom pointed out, "A couple of Jews here and there." We had agreed we would sell her house and have her move in by March 2007. It was a good decision. We had a great relationship. She was still very easy to talk to and have fun with—and make fun of, all in good nature.

That summer, we went out to the Hamptons to visit friends we had meet the previous year on a cruise to Asia. They had a Westie (West Highland Terrier) and I fell in love with it. Hope and I had argued about dogs and could never decide so late that December, Lori and Jeff and the boys showed up at our house with a puppy and handed it to us, saying: " You can't decide so we decided for you." It was a white fur, brown eared Cockapoo, we named Latke. After all, we got him for Chanukah. Hope said she had never seen me so happy and animated, obviously something that had disappeared over the years, though I didn't think so. Latke and I bonded and all this parental love that had been missing for a long time, was now directed at this new member of the household. Shortly after, we went to Starbucks with Latke and a couple outside remarked: "We had a Cockapoo who died. We've got to tell you, it's like losing a child." I thought : No way! This is way TOO easy, but Hope dug her nails into my arm and said:"don't go there." I didn't.

Ten months later, Lori and Jeff would surprise us again, with a black and white cockapoo who we named Farfel and there we were, the four of us, with a new kind of family, albeit it different by conventional standards but there was no doubt there was a lot of love flowing in a house that had been joyless in some ways for way too long. Regardless, I would have loved to have shown the Starbucks couple earlier, that it was nothing like having-and perhaps losing-a child.

Less than a week later though, another lifecycle would fall upon me.

In early December, Hope and I agreed to go to Miami for New Year's to usher in 2007 at Alan and Amy's. Over the years, we had become closer, and Hope and Amy were sisters-in-law who genuinely liked each other. Each was fiercely independent and obstinate, but the Kluger boys were no walk in the park either.

Our flight was scheduled for December 30, and we planned to go down for a few days. Alan called me early the morning of December 28. My mom had been found unconscious in her living room, wearing a white tennis outfit, a tennis racquet in her left hand, a pack of Marlboros just out of reach of the right.

She had fallen into a coma and was unresponsive. By the time we got to Miami at 6:00 that evening, she was being kept alive on a respirator. That night, we went out for Italian food and decided to disconnect her from life support.

Alan and I had been sitting in the waiting room together for about thirty minutes when the doctor came out and said she was gone. I was now officially an orphan. I didn't cry. I hadn't cried for my dad. Maybe I was becoming a pro at this, or maybe it just didn't rock my world the way Erica's death had.

But it meant another funeral and another speech. This time, Alan had the good sense to go before me.

Eulogy for Mom, December 30, 2006
by Barry Kluger
Remember the Robbins Vaccine? How about the famous Kroll Game Company. Do you recall someone yelling "give him Safar" when someone stopped breathing?

Probably not. Dr. Frederick Robbins found a way to cultivate the polio virus in a tissue culture, preceding the development of the Salk and Sabin vaccines. Fred Kroll invented the games Trouble and Hungry, Hungry Hippo for the Kohner and Hasbro Companies. Dr. Peter Safar combined mouth-to-mouth resuscitation with closed-chest cardiac compression that came to be known as CPR. And while they were not very well known, they left legacies behind.

How does one measure a year in a life? According to the Broadway hit *Rent,* it's 525,600 minutes and can be measured in daylights, in sunsets, in midnights, in cups of coffee.

This is a fan letter of sorts to my mom. She didn't invent a vaccine, a board game, or beat on my chest … well, she did just a few times, but if I had waited to note her contribution until we all read it in a paper, I would have done a disservice to her and myself, depriving ourselves of a most wonderful thing: reaching out and touching someone when they were alive and around to hear our words. And I did my best to remind her—and myself—every day.

My success as a person is due to nurturing. Not in that coddling "Let me make that decision for you" kind of parenting, but rather, "let me give you the tools to succeed or fail," and if you stumble, I am here to provide a compass, NOT a get-out-of-jail-free card.

In *The Wizard of Oz,* the Wizard tells the Tin Man a heart is not measured by how much you love but by how much you are loved by others. Look at this place today. And you know she's taking attendance.

Every conversation with my mother began … Hi … It's me … hang on. I got another call … hello?? No Mom, it's me. Oh … okay … hang on … click … hello? Yeah, Mom, it's still me … Okay. I think I lost Esta-Dara … Esta Dara? … No, Mom, still Barry.

Last week, I was talking to my mom, and she asked if I was calling from my car because she hates when I talk on the phone while driving. I said, "Geez, you are a pain in the ass." She said, "I'm still your mother." I replied "I'm fifty-two, Mom!" She paused and said, "You're fifty-two? Gee, I must be older than I thought."

My house was full of laughs, love, and as most of you know, a lot of antique crap. The Metropolitan Museum couldn't hold a candle to the Lee Kluger Collection.

They say part of life is death. I guess I am tired of taking out my black suit … for my dad, for my mom, and for Erica. I am tired of missing Artie, George, Mack, Hank, Henry, Ida, Phil, Hilda, Izzie, and everyone else.

But that is what they call the lifecycle. But it doesn't mean we have to like it. But we do have to live with it and learn from it and grow and love more deeply from it.

John Lennon said, "Life is what happens when you're busy making other plans." But I think Paul McCartney said it better: "And in the end, the love you take is equal to the love you make."

My mom was real. She spoke the plain truth, and she didn't care what people thought. They knew she was a friend for life. She wasn't just my mother. She was my best friend.

My mom had a life, not a career. She is remembered, and boy, oh boy, did she make a difference.

We got to ride The Lee Train. It was a helluva ride. It stopped everywhere, and it picked up passengers along the way, me … you, you, and you.

And somewhere, the ride continues, and I am sure that if there's a place you go next, my mom is bumming a cigarette, dad is flipping the channels, and Erica is loving her grandparents "oodles and oodles of Chinese noodles."

We all became better people for those we let touch us and come into our lives. She brought me and all of us into hers, and, for that, I will be forever grateful.

Chapter 33

Death Touches a Friend

E-mail to an old colleague
October 26, 2007

Dear Nicole,

I am embarrassed and disappointed in myself for not having reached out when you lost your daughter. I, more than anyone, having lost Erica, should have known how important it was to be surrounded by friends, family, and associates at that very difficult time. I had lunch yesterday here in Scottsdale with Sluggo, who filled me in on general stuff and relayed the story of how Susan, Patty, and Roberta came to be with you. I e-mailed Roberta for your address.

Nicole, I hate the fact we belong to this club that no one wants to join because the cost of admission is too high. Almost seven years later, I still scratch at that scab, and it remains fresh. Part of that is to insure we will never forget.

I wish you love and peace, and hope you live the kind of life your daughter would have wanted to live and would have wanted you to live. Forgive me for not being there. Feel free to call if you ever want to talk.

With love,

Barry

October 28, 2007

Dear Barry,

Please don't be embarrassed—as you know so well, I have hardly been able to respond and answer cards, calls, and notes anyway! I remember very well when Erica died and how horrified I was for your pain and loss. I couldn't even imagine what it would be like to lose a child, and what you must have been going through was incomprehensible to me at the time.

Now I understand it all too well. I miss my Dominique every minute, and I still can't believe that I won't hug her and talk to her. I find myself calling her voicemail, which I can't bear to disconnect, just to hear her voice. To not have been able to take away her pain is so very difficult. I just don't know when I'll get through this, or if I ever really will—I suppose not. They say I'll learn to see the beauty in things again and feel some of my old optimism, but it all seems a bit unattainable now.

It has been six months, and it still feels like yesterday. I keep having that vision of her in the morgue, and the feeling that I had when I got the call just won't go away. How did you get beyond the acute pain? Is it really just the passage of time?

I was so touched that Roberta, Patty, and Susan came to stay with me. MTVN was filled with so much warmth and friendship way back then ... that certainly changed! Mark has also been a good friend.

How are you, and by the way, what are you up to these days? How do you make it through the holidays? Thanksgiving was so hard—I kept trying to remind myself to be grateful for every minute I had with her, but I just kept feeling that it wasn't even close to enough.

Thanks, Barry, for reaching out. I truly am touched.
Love,
Nicole

December 28, 2007
Barry,
Our daughter, Erica, died November 29, 2007. She was nineteen. We are dealing with our loss as best we know how. I Googled "Erica, death." I found your viewpoint, and it resonates in my own. The sense of loss is immeasurable.

The size of the hole in my heart feels like it can never be filled again. I have a loving and supportive wife. Together with our two older sons we will find our direction.
Thank you for sharing,
Eric (a dad who has lost a daughter and found me on the Internet)

Chapter 34

Closure? Perhaps

In April 2008, I had organized a reunion of my high school social network, a group of more than eighty who saw at least some mixture of the gang every day or weekend during tenth, eleventh, and twelfth grades. Back in 2006, when my mom died, we went through her stuff and found the engagement ring I had given Carol. Carol had class and had returned it my mother, stone intact, since it was a setting that had been in the family.

I wanted to give the setting to my niece, Lisa, but couldn't decide what to do with the stone. I asked Hope if she wanted me to make something out of it for her. In her typical deadpan way, she said, "A one-carat diamond? What am I going to do with a one-carat diamond?" implying sarcastically that it was too small for her taste. After deciding that an earring was a bit too "midlife crisis-like" for me, I decided I would give it to Erica's half-sister Alexandra (Alley).

I made plans to see Erica's stepdad, Matt, when I was on Long Island for the reunion and give it to him. He called me and told me he was on his way into the city with Carol and Alley and that they would see me at the hotel. "They?" I had not seen Carol since the funeral seven years earlier, and we had spoken maybe twice over the years. Once Erica was gone, there seemed to be no reason for us to speak, and it was difficult for her to get back to a new kind of normalcy that I had so easily, or so I thought, resumed.

Matt, Hope, and I had shared e-mails over the years on anniversaries, and we asked how the kids were and exchanged some updates, even some humor. But Carol and I had not reached that point.

As they drove up to the hotel, I walked to their car, and said my hellos. I hugged Carol. It was awkward but not without true affection on my part. After all, she had done nothing wrong in our marriage to warrant my leaving, and I had always felt bad about the pain I had caused her—and most of all, Erica.

We sat in the lobby bar and spent some time catching up. I took out the stone and gave it to Alley. I told her that, in a different life, this ring would have been Erica's. She thanked me. I walked them to their car, and they left.

I got on the phone to Hope to tell her how it had gone, and without any warning—or expectation—I broke down sobbing and couldn't stop. Just then, a few of my friends from high school drove up, and Shelley, whom I had had a crush on since I was twelve, came up and just hugged me.

I didn't think I needed closure, and I don't believe you ever get closure but rather acceptance, in some way. Carol and I had had what I thought would likely be our last meeting, but it brought me full circle and closed a chapter of pain that I hadn't thought existed.

But it felt so good. Life and death come in many stages. This was one more stage, seven years later.

June 2008

Dear Carol and family,

I just wanted to take a moment to tell you how proud and honored I am that Jessica was chosen to receive the Erica Kluger Dance Scholarship, and why it is so special to her. You might remember that I used to work in the office back when Mrs. Stroud owned the studio and Erica was a Senior Company member. I would have the pleasure of her company, complete with infectious grin and impish demeanor, several times each week. My son, Richie, was little then and used to come to work with me ... Erica would delight in telling Richie how cute he was and how she was going to marry him one day—and even though he would get thoroughly flustered, she definitely made quite an impression because he remembers those moments to this day.

You might also know that I lost my husband at an early age, when Jessica was four and Richie was two—and thus, I have spent a lot of hours pondering the fairness of life, as I'm sure you have.

I think one of the universal fears when we lose a loved one is that somehow they will be forgotten as time goes on ... but I just wanted you to know that I, we, could never forget the beautiful, special young lady that Erica was, and I feel privileged that we were able to know her.

Peace and love to you all,

T.H.

April 6, 2009

Hello Barry,

You may or may not remember me, my name is Jimmy and I was very close with Erica. You and I met a few times when Erica and I were younger, but I know it is probably hard to remember everyone she was close with since it seemed like she was friends with the whole town.

I know today is probably as tough as can be for you each year it passes. April 6 is never easy for me either. Erica was one of the most important people in my life from the time she moved to Setauket in fifth grade up until that awful day eight years ago, and really, she still plays an important part in my life today.

I always read her obituary on this morning and look through some pictures I have of her smiling face and, somehow, I saw your e-mail address tagged to one of the obituary links; I thought I would drop you a line and let you know how much she meant to me and all of her other friends as well as let you know that my thoughts are with you and your family on what I am sure is a most difficult day.

On the first day Erica came into Mrs. Francis's fifth-grade class, I knew she was someone I needed to get to know. She had a certain uniqueness to her that was unlike many of the other people in that school. It took her a while to get warmed up to me and Sarah but, eventually, she came around and we became very close. Throughout that year, we formed a very strong bond that would last forever. I will never forget, one day in sixth grade, Erica and I were talking, and she said she wanted to go to her senior prom with me. She said she would never change her mind, no matter what, and that was final. I said something like, "Yeah, right, you'll never remember that six years from now," and thought nothing of it.

When I reached eleventh grade, I moved to another school, and Erica and I remained close. One day, senior year, I got a phone call from her, and she said she had a very important question ... she wanted to ask me to the prom. I was floored, I couldn't believe she remembered, let alone still wanted to take me. I already had another date but told her to "get lost" in favor of your beautiful daughter; I'm sure you would agree it was a good move. That story is just one example of how genuine Erica was and how lucky I felt to have her as a friend.

Through the years, Erica and I had a great friendship. She was my first "girlfriend," first kiss, my prom date, my own personal comedian, and just a beacon of fun and happiness in my life from the first day I met her. I truly loved your daughter as one of my best friends, and I will never forget her wonderful smile and personality. I know you probably have not talked to a lot of her friends about her and probably have not heard many of us give you our views of our relationship with her.

I hope this message finds you well and you are not upset that I contacted you. I know that Erica always talked so fondly about you, and I thought it might help to hear some kind words about your wonderful daughter. She was always so excited when she talked about you, and it seemed to me that you and she had a very special relationship. I have many pictures and things that I would be happy to share with you if you like.

Feel free to reach out if you would like me to send you some of the photos I have of her with her friends. It may not be something you want to discuss, and I completely understand if that is the case. Again, I am sorry if this was an e-mail you would have rather not received. Erica truly influenced my life in a great way, and I can assure you, if nothing else, that she will always be in my thoughts, and I will do my best to make sure myself and her other friends continue to do our best to remember her life and make sure her name lives on through her scholarship fund.

All the best,

James

In the summer of 2009, my niece, Lisa, sent me a copy of the program of the wedding of Erica's friend, Samara, whom Erica last saw in the late 1990s. In it, Samara remembered the relatives who had passed, and she remembered Erica.

Chapter 35

Erica Turns Twenty-seven: The Words of Others

November is the second hardest month of the year, after April. It's the time I count in my head, and on my fingers, how old Erica would have been on November 27. It usually falls at Thanksgiving, so, while it is a holiday to give thanks for what we have, it is also a time to reflect on what we have lost.

November 2009 was extra special. It was the month we found out my sister-in-law had stage-one breast cancer, but all the follow-up tests showed there was no spread. It was also the month that Hope was declared "clean" in her mammograms and genetic testing. It truly was a time to give thanks.

Shannon and I exchanged e-mails and I asked her to recall Erica, the good and the bad and not sugarcoat it. In Shannon's world, this was her life with Erica.

Erica—my baby, my sister, my friend. Erica was amazing. We were blessed enough to have Camp Danbee. The promotional video for the camp says it's a place where girls can kick further, sing louder, fly higher, and make friends that will last a lifetime. That is exactly what it was. We were little girls to anyone else but to us, we just were.

Shannon, Erica, Jade, and Samara. We called our group "The Quadrant." We had a little nook in our senior year ski lodge–style bunk and we sectioned it off from the rest of the girls. So many memories, where do I start?

Erica was boy-crazy, she was sweet, loving, and funny and playful. One of my memories from camp, we were on a trip, and we got in trouble for jumping out of the window of our hotel room, crossing the street, hopping a fence, and jumping in the pool of someone across the street … with the boys. We swam in our underwear. It was crazy. We didn't get caught, but I was stupid enough to show our counselors the pictures. Erica and I were banned from going to a concert. But they actually gave me this fun memory with Erica alone just to bond and have fun together. We went on top of the "mess hall" where we were preparing for our end-of-the-year themed banquet. We spent the night writing our names on the wall in paint and seeing the other names that were so old on the wall and realizing we were lucky to be part of a long tradition of campers. We made up dances together, and it was just so nice to hang out with her.

I was so excited when I found out that Erica would be in Arizona with her father while I was attending ASU. It was very scary for me to imagine going all the way across the country by myself knowing not that many people. We spent almost the whole year hanging out together. We called ourselves "frat rats." I hadn't seen Erica in years, and I remember she pulled up in this red Honda Civic, which at the time to me was a big deal and looked like a hot car. She had this new short haircut and a new nose. She was gorgeous. She was totally a cute kid, but now she was a beautiful young woman. She exuded this confidence that was unmistakable at the time. I was so insecure and stressed about being away from home, and I had her to lean on. She was confident, beautiful, funny, happy, and ready to party. She would take me in her car on the highway, and she lit a cigarette at certain street lights … that was her routine.

One night, we wanted to go out and really didn't know anyone, so we went to the fraternities. We were so nervous, like Dorothy knocking on the Wizard's door. We knocked, and this guy (I'll name him Chad) opened the door. He took one look at Erica, and the rest is history. We were at that fraternity like every night. Swimming, hanging out in their room, joking around. Chad and Erica were boyfriend/girlfriend in no time. She wanted me to date his roommate so badly, but there was something about two guys having a leopard-print ironing board that I just could not shake. They were also so different from the East Coast boys that I was used to. But turns out the leopard print was nothing to worry about.

Erica loved him so much. They were really cute together. I was a bit jealous, actually. But we had fun. We would play Notorious B.I.G. and rap all the words. We'd play it at the frats and in her car—that was our theme song together. Then one day we walked into one of our friend's dorm rooms when they weren't expecting us, and there were drugs around. They tried to hide it, but it was too late. We had already seen it. It was the first time I had ever seen it. It seemed the same way for Erica too. I think that had an influence on her because she looked up to him and loved him so much. Time went on, and Chad's attention started to decrease in intensity toward Erica. This was slowly starting to affect her. She got this job at a restaurant where the people there were also a bad influence on her. The manager had a wife but had a girlfriend at the restaurant that he would hold hands with at parties and hook up with.

One weekend, Erica's parents went away, and we decided to have people over. So I was going to sleep over there both nights. The first night, it was all my friends from school, and it was a blast. The second night, it wasn't so fun because it was all her people from work. I remember spending the whole night in her bedroom not wanting to come out because I did not like these people at all—I did not like the guy cheating on his wife, and there was something "bad news" about these people. I felt like a party-pooper. But Erica would occasionally come in and check on me. Erica increasingly became more and more of a party girl. She was, as her father says, "The life of the party," but it was starting to become reckless. I kept telling her Chad was not good for her or right for her. She loved him—you can't talk to someone who was in love. I hated him for her. I hated that he was having such a power over her and making her want to be like him. I also started to feel like she didn't really care to hang out with me but just have me to come with her to see him. Everything was about him. But their relationship changed. One day, Chad started dating a girl in my sorority. I wanted Erica to get him out of her mind once and for all, so I took pictures of him with his new girlfriend, and I showed them to her. This is something I do regret doing. But I wanted her to be over it and move on with her life. She saw the pictures, and I could see that I hurt her very badly by showing them to her. Tears came out of her eyes, and I felt horrible. This is all very blurry to me now, being that it was like almost nine years ago.

One night she rode up to my apartment, wanting to go see him. It was a school night for me, and I tried to explain to her that I could not go out. She looked at me desperately and said, "Please, Shannon, I'm going to do something stupid if I don't see him." It was then that I realized something had to be done. I realized the control of this boy and/or the lifestyle was taking over her, and she was becoming a victim. I called Erica's dad the next day (March 2 to be exact) and told him what was going on. He came right home from his vacation and put her into rehab. She was getting better, she was grounded, but she *was* getting better. I couldn't see her for a month. She was finally getting back on track, and she had a new job. She was getting structure, what she always needed. Then I spoke to her, and she told me how things were really doing a lot better and she was getting along with Hope, her stepmom. She was really happy about that, and things were looking up. She said she was finally ungrounded. I was so excited and asked her to come down to campus and visit me. She said she was going to get some blond highlights and wanted to wait because she didn't want Chad to see her until she got the highlights, and I was really kind of hurt. I was hurt that it was all about him. She was finally ungrounded and wouldn't come see me just to hang out with me. The power of love or obsession was still taking hold. The last thing I said to Erica was, "You're pathetic," and she kind of laughed and said, "I know."

About a month after she had come home, I was in my dorm room, and Barry, her dad, called me. He said, "Hi, Shannon." I knew. I kept blabbing, hoping that he would keep talking to me like nothing was wrong, but his "Hi, Shannon" said it all. And then he said it. I screamed so loud my dorm thought someone was murdered. I've had a lot of people I know die in my life, but nothing hurt as much as this. I loved her so much and cared about her so much. I felt like I was always watching out for her like a mother. And I hadn't even seen her in a month. She was always walking on thin ice and playing with fire, but to die in a freak car accident? It didn't make sense. She was just on her way to work. She wasn't drinking and driving, she wasn't on drugs. I don't even think she had her phone because her dad took it away. I can't make any sense of it. I think she knows how much I loved her. I hate what my last words to her were. People always say to you to tell the people you love that you love them because you never know what the last thing you'll say to them will be. It's true. I was being selfish and jealous.

At her father's house after the funeral, her dad gave me an envelope that said "Shannon" on it. I opened it. It was a letter from Erica. She had written it during the month she had come home, and she thanked me for telling her dad, and told me she loved me. I felt like she was speaking to me. I thought it was so weird that she had written me this letter, because it wasn't like her. It was very out of character, and it was the first time I felt like she cared about me and really did realize how much I cared about her. She taught me a lot and gave me a greater appreciation of life and the loved ones and the time we have here.

My memories of Erica are real, not sugarcoated. It's just the way it was. If people take away something from Erica's death, it would be that you have to keep your eyes on the road every second you are behind the wheel. There is something I've kept to myself. There is something I never really shared. I called her dad about her problems. I tried to take care of her with her boyfriend, but the thing that killed her was an automobile. The one thing I never thought to address. She was a bad driver. There were many times I would be in the car with her, and we escaped death time and time again, and she would laugh and say, "We're all gonna die." There were cigarettes, there was a cell phone, there was music, and makeup. There are so many things we can distract ourselves with in a car. The only difference between us and Erica is one split second.

She was on a road to recovery, literally on her way to her new job, getting better, doing better ... things were looking up. It didn't have to end this way. The road is like a war zone, and we should all treat it that way every time we get behind the wheel. I want to say nothing but good things about Erica. She was an amazingly beautiful girl with a loving personality who was magnetic and funny—she had the world at her fingertips.

Erica, I'm sorry, and I love you so much. I think about you every day and every time I see the bunny tattoo I have. I know you can't believe I was actually at the Playboy Mansion out here in L.A. as I work on my acting career, and I told Hef about you. He was touched. We'll always have Danbee, and we'll always have freshman year. And ... we will always have each other.
Xoxoxox
Love,
Shannon

November was also a time that Erica's Aunt Ellen wrote me to apologize for not writing something for this book. Her apology was the chapter I was looking for.

Ya know I was putzing around on the computer and I started to read all your articles that you have written and I know you had asked me to write a little about Erica and I never did. Not that I did not want to but every time I think of her and started to, my kids are always by me and ask me why I am crying. It is very hard to explain to them about Erica and how much she meant to me as they did not get the opportunity to know her. But what they do know about her is how happy she made me every time I saw her. I tell them that she was such a funny kid.

Soooo funny that she made me belly laugh every time I saw her. I was a teenage kid who was out all the time, but when I knew that Erica was coming, all was dropped for her! I enjoyed every moment that I got to spend with her! Every single one! From the minute she got to Gram's and "Pop-Up's" house, we never knew what we were in for but we knew it was going to be fun!

First thing was to know if my brother, Neil, was home … oh, and if he was, she was in heaven! But if he wasn't, she would be sure to run up to his room to open the door so she could at least smell him!!!!! His room stunk, she didn't care! She just loved Neil! The more he pushed her outta his room, the more she loved him! So funny!

We did not have to entertain her in any way as she was always the entertainment! She is the one who taught us all how to steam a large spoon with our breath and stick it on our nose and it stayed!!! For God's sake she taught half of Andra's wedding to do it! She went table to table! Speaking of Andra's wedding, did I ever tell you that as she went from table to table for spoon lessons, she proceeded to take each disposable camera from the table as she got there and climb under the table and take pictures of everyone from under the table!!!! When Andra got all her cameras developed, they weren't of scenes from her wedding; they were pictures of people knees, under their dresses and of the spoon lessons and each one who got the spoon to stay!

You know that Erica named my first son Joseph. He was Jake for the first twenty-four hours. And she was one of the first ones to see him and told me he looked like a Joey! I have it all on video … she just kept calling him Joey! Ten years later, still Joey! I wish he would have known her … he would have loved her so much too! My Alex is named after her as he is Alexander Eric (she was Erica Alexis) and I think that he is just as much a "scootch" as she was! She was one in a million, no other like her, beautiful, funny and loved more than ever and will forever be missed by all that knew her.

I just wanted you to really know how much I miss her, loved her and will never forget her. Erica's death had a huge impact on my life and even though she was not my biological niece, I couldn't love her more if I tried. I am so sorry for your loss every day and I hope it brings joy to you to know how much she meant to me.
Love,
Ellen

I got Facebooked by Erica's friends from Long Island. I last saw these kids as eighteen-year-old high school grads. Now they were twenty-seven-year-olds, with jobs, some with marriages, but grown up in many ways and still kids in others. Devon, Katie C. and Katie D., Holly, Lauren, Kelley, and Jenna posted comments about the photos I had in my online album and shared their laughs, stories, and sadness.

Devon e-mailed me her thoughts.

Erica Alexis Kluger
Every time I hear or say your name, I smile. You were the most sincere, kindest, and sweetest person I've ever known. When you left for Arizona after high school graduation, I knew I didn't get a chance to say goodbye, but I didn't think I had to. I thought I'd see you again.

You were my oldest friend. You always knew how to make everyone laugh; you had a contagiously beautiful smile and an effortless way about you. You also had some random memories that you'd share with me occasionally and remind me of what a bully I was in elementary school, the "GET ME THE KETCHUP" story, or any other time I bossed you around. I was mean, and you still stuck around.

You were the greatest big sister. You cared so much for Zack and Alley, always hugging and kissing them. They were always invited everywhere and anywhere you went with your friends. They adored you too.

You always had the coolest stuff! Colorful neat clothes, awesome multi-color paint-splashed Nickelodeon sneakers—always fashionable, even at eight years old.

I remember us dancing in my backyard around my pool to Moxy Fruvus—*Once I Was the King of Spain*. You would dance a few steps, and then crack up, while the rest of us were already on the ground laughing. We traveled to Italy together in seventh grade with our Latin class and, boy, was I homesick. But you got me through it.

You were also BOY-crazy! But painfully shy about it. You started the "Who Likes Who" wall in my bathroom and consistently updated it from middle school through high school. I was going to paint my bathroom walls a few years ago, but I can't bear to cover your writing. You playfully threatened Lisa for liking the same boy as you and wrote her a message next to her "Who Likes Who" section, "Lisa, you better not like Barry or I'll beat you up."

You wouldn't hurt a fly. You had a GUM TRAY. That remained a secret … until now. You also made graffiti on my bathroom wall with a height chart. You always were the shortest. And you made sure to write "Erica Kluger" with your exact height measurement.

We went to senior prom as juniors with great guys. They were good friends, so it was fun for us to get ready together, take prom pictures together, and have a blast with good people! We changed into our dresses at my house; you never picked up your clothes. I still have your worn, gray *Les Miserables* T-shirt and khaki pants. You always seemed to leave a "trail" everywhere you went.

I see you in my dreams sometimes. You seem so real. I never got to say goodbye, I miss you and think of you often. I catch myself in thoughts of you. "What would you have become?" "Where would you be today?" I think of all the people that have come through my life and say to myself, "They would've LOVED you, Erica." What a special person you are, and always will be. I will forever remember you with a smile on my face.

It was also this time I got another e-mail from Erica's senior prom date, Jimmy.

November 10, 2009
Hey Barry,
I am terribly sorry it took me so long to get back to you. I thought I had replied to this a while ago but just realized it was caught up in my "drafts" folder, I feel like an ass.

Anyway, I would love to chat sometime. I think it's great that you spend time talking with Erica at the cemetery; I often find myself talking to the picture I have of her on my desk when I'm in the weeds at work or dealing with some struggles. Erica, more than maybe anyone else I have ever known, always managed to get a laugh or a smile out of me, and I'm guessing a lot of that comes from you.

I am currently trying to pursue a career singing in addition to my day job, and when I am writing songs, I get a lot of inspiration from my memories of your daughter. I hope to get back in the studio soon to record some of my songs and, if any of the Erica-inspired tracks make the cut, I will be sure to pass them on to you.

If you are ever in NYC, please let me know. I would love to grab a bite or a beer and meet with you face-to-face, if you have the time. Additionally, I have been meaning to get out to Arizona in order to visit with Erica, and I am hoping to do so this winter … perhaps we can hit the golf course if I ever make it down there.

I hope all is well.
Regards,
Jimmy

Erica's childhood friend Katie wrote a poem.

Erica Alexis, Our Sweet Girl

Glowing Erica,
drawing others to you,
with your warmth,
and irresistible charm.

Sweet, pure memories,
of times spent with you….

Tickets at American Video, treks to West Meadow Beach, Jesse at Starbucks, Brad Renfro, crushes we thought would last forever, Spice Girls, Backstreet Boys, the scent of Tommy Hilfiger, Bug Juice, Carrot toes, endless nicknames, Broken joints, and our broken hearts.

And laughing, always laughing….

Even in tears, thoughts of you bring forth a smile.

Your life's joys, sprinkled like seeds,
bloom flowers in the garden of life.

Knowing you, so enchanting,
to those you touched,
your imprint is eternal.

This November 27, my nephew, Jesse, called from Florida. Jesse has always marched to his own beat, sometimes to the consternation of his family, but uncles are always good for a hall pass. Now a lawyer on his own terms, he said, "Uncle Barry, I know I have kind of been off the radar for a few years but I just wanted to tell you I know today is Erica's birthday and just wanted to see how you're doing." There is no way to know what Erica meant to him, but I got a good idea.

Chapter 36

2010: Looking Back

Toward the end of December 2009, I got a letter from Carol. We had never really spoken about Erica since she died almost nine years earlier. All I will say is her words gave me great comfort and filled me with a sense of love for someone who had been my wife and Erica's mother. The grace and tenderness shone through. I know Erica would have carried that quality throughout her life, had she had the chance.

Over the years, I have given up on trying to make sense of Erica's death. There is no sense to it. It just happened. God doesn't cause car accidents. I tried to convey to people what it's like when you get the news. While each case of dealing with death is different, it wasn't until I saw *Mystic River* in 2003 that I understand what I had felt that day in 2001. In the movie, the character played by Sean Penn finds out his daughter has been murdered. He collapses, wanting to scream, but nothing comes out. This scene captures the feeling. See that scene and you get an idea what it's like. It is so deep inside that maybe self-preservation is what keeps it there for the moment. For some unknown reason, our bodies and our hearts protect us. Maybe our bodies and minds release only what we can handle at that instance.

Movies are amazing triggers for emotion. *The Princess Diaries* is one film I wish Erica had seen. It is about fairytale love for a young teenage girl and a fantasy I had hoped Erica would experience. I gather she did feel that with her first real boyfriend here in Arizona.

And I found out the feeling was mutual. The First week of March, I received a letter from her boyfriend, at the time of her death. He wrote:

> Dear Barry: I remember summer 2000 in Tempe, Arizona. Dorms were filling up with new students and old friends were seeing one another after a long summer apart. Never would I have dreamed that after I finished unpacking, I would walk downstairs to meet an exceptionally amazing person. Erica was wearing all white, with a dark tan, short brown hair, piercing blue eyes and smile that lit up the room. She was all I could focus on that night and all I thought about for the next several months.
>
> She was young and innocent and gave everyone a fair chance. She taught me that McDonalds serves #2 without meat, how to have fun doing just about anything at anytime, about the bond you can share with a friend or with your family, and that nothing will ever break it. Erica had grace and style and she wore her heart on her sleeve. There will never be another like her again. In her passing I learned so much about what I wanted to do with in life, how there are things that you will never be able to take back, and how I

would like people to remember me. I hope someone will remember me as I remember Erica, an Angel.
Be well,
Chad

Over the years, Hope and I have built a full life—full of laughs, adventures, and lots of "Erica would love this" or "that's something Erica would do."

The scab has grown over the wound, and I pick at it now and then. But not so much. I don't feel guilty that I shed fewer tears. But regular visits to the cemetery give me pause and make me wonder where the years have gone. I divide my life into two parts: life with Erica and life without.

But the continuous thread of emotion is what sustains us, and it's all part of "life."

Over the years, the memories of those we have lost grow a little stronger, but the recollections grow a little dimmer.

Grief is, indeed, a team sport. It involves everyone who was touched by Erica. We live so that people will always remember those moments, and we tell them to our families, our friends, the lady at Starbucks, the guy at the supermarket. We talk of our loss, first with deep pain and, as the years go by, with celebration.

Erica was a person to celebrate. I celebrate her every day. I remember her every day. And I miss her every day. Yet somehow, the person I have become and hope to become, before my time ends, stems from the innocence and love that was Erica. If I can view the world as she did, then it will always be a sunny day for me.

I am reminded of the saying, "A life lived in fear, is a life half-lived." Erica was fearless, and she lived life to its fullest.

About The Author

Barry Kluger is a corporate communications and public relations executive with more than thirty years of experience with some of the world's most recognizable brands and companies. He has served in senior management at USA Networks, MTV Networks, and Prodigy. He is managing partner of Kluger Media Group, LLC, a public relations firm (www.barrykluger.com). Kluger is a regular contributing columnist to Gannett's *Arizona Republic, Jewish News of Phoenix,* and other publications. He lives with his wife, Hope Kirsch, an attorney, and their dogs, Latke and Farfel, in Scottsdale, Arizona. He still goes to the cemetery weekly with a pitching wedge and a couple of golf balls. He talks to Erica. And she talks back.

Manufactured By: RR Donnelley
Breinigsville, PA USA
April 2010